D1417793

Life on
Alcatraz

Titles in The Way People Live series include:

Cowboys in the Old West
Games of Ancient Rome
Life Aboard an African Slave Ship
Life Among the Great Plains Indians
Life Among the Ibo Women of Nigeria
Life Among the Indian Fighters
Life Among the Pirates
Life Among the Samurai
Life Among the Vikings
Life During the Black Death
Life During the Crusades
Life During the French Revolution
Life During the Gold Rush
Life During the Great Depression
Life During the Middle Ages
Life During the Renaissance
Life During the Russian Revolution
Life During the Spanish Inquisition
Life in a Japanese American Internment Camp
Life in a Medieval Castle
Life in Ancient Athens
Life in Ancient Greece
Life in Ancient Rome
Life in an Eskimo Village
Life in a Wild West Show
Life in Charles Dickens's England
Life in the Amazon Rain Forest
Life in the American Colonies
Life in the Elizabethan Theater
Life in the Hitler Youth
Life in the North During the Civil War
Life in the South During the Civil War
Life in the Warsaw Ghetto
Life in Victorian England
Life in War-Torn Bosnia
Life of a Roman Slave
Life of a Roman Soldier
Life of a Slave on a Southern Plantation
Life on a Medieval Pilgrimage
Life on Alcatraz
Life on an Israeli Kibbutz
Life on Ellis Island
Life on the American Frontier
Life on the Oregon Trail
Life on the Underground Railroad
Life Under the Jim Crow Laws

THE WAY
PEOPLE
LIVE

Life on
Alcatraz

by Judith Janda Presnall

Lucent Books, P.O. Box 289011, San Diego, CA 92198-9011

Acknowledgments

Three people were special in helping me assemble information for this book: Frank Heaney, a former correctional officer at the federal penitentiary on Alcatraz answered many questions; Richard Craig, a pilot friend provided a spectacular view of the island prison from the air; and Lance Presnall, my husband who cheerfully photographs all my requests and happily supports all my writing endeavors.

Library of Congress Cataloging-in-Publication Data

Presnall, Judith Janda.
  Life on Alcatraz / by Judith Janda Presnall.
      p. cm. — (The way people live)
Includes bibliographical references and index.
Summary: Discusses the prison on Alcatraz Island, California, otherwise known as the "Rock," describing the cell house, the routine of prison life, inmates' leisure time, breaking prison rules, employee and family life, closing Alcatraz prison, and the island's future roles.
  ISBN 1-56006-639-3 (hard : alk. paper)
  1. United States Penitentiary, Alcatraz Island, California—Juvenile literature. 2. Alcatraz Island (Calif.)—History—Juvenile literature. [1. United States Penitentiary, Alcatraz Island, California. 2. Alcatraz Island (Calif.)—History. 3. Prisons—History.] I. Title. II. Series.
  HV9474.A4 P74 2001
  365'.979461—dc21

                                                          00-008056

Cover photo: As photographers record the event, the last inmates of Alcatraz Federal Penitentiary leave the prison on March 21st, 1963.

To prison personnel and inmates—
for an improved future

Contents

FOREWORD
Discovering the Humanity in Us All   8

INTRODUCTION
Criminals Must Be Separated from Society   10

CHAPTER ONE
A Tough Prison for Tough Criminals   12

CHAPTER TWO
Arriving on the Rock: A Life Like No Other   23

CHAPTER THREE
The Cell House   35

CHAPTER FOUR
Routine, Routine, Routine   46

CHAPTER FIVE
Inmates' Leisure Time: Life by the Book   56

CHAPTER SIX
Breaking Prison Rules   66

CHAPTER SEVEN
Employee and Family Life on the Rock   78

CHAPTER EIGHT
Closing Alcatraz Prison: The Island's Future Roles   90

Notes   100
For Further Reading   103
Works Consulted   104
Index   106
Picture Credits   111
About the Author   112

Discovering the Humanity in Us All

Books in The Way People Live series focus on groups of people in a wide variety of circumstances, settings, and time periods. Some books focus on different cultural groups, others, on people in a particular historical time period, while others cover people involved in a specific event. Each book emphasizes the daily routines, personal and historical struggles, and achievements of people from all walks of life.

To really understand any culture, it is necessary to strip the mind of the common notions we hold about groups of people. These stereotypes are the archenemies of learning. It does not even matter whether the stereotypes are positive or negative; they are confining and tight. Removing them is a challenge that's not easily met, as anyone who has ever tried it will admit. Ideas that do not fit into the templates we create are unwelcome visitors—ones we would prefer remain quietly in a corner or forgotten room.

The cowboy of the Old West is a good example of such confining roles. The cowboy was courageous, yet soft-spoken. His time (it is always a he, in our template) was spent alternatively saving a rancher's daughter from certain death on a runaway stagecoach, or shooting it out with rustlers. At times, of course, he was likely to get a little crazy in town after a trail drive, but for the most part, he was the epitome of inner strength. It is disconcerting to find out that the cowboy is human, even a bit childish. Can it really be true that cowboys would line up to help the cook on the trail drive grind coffee, just hoping he would give them a little stick of peppermint candy that came with the coffee shipment? The idea of tough cowboys vying with one another to help "Coosie" (as they called their cooks) for a bit of candy seems silly and out of place.

So is the vision of Eskimos playing video games and watching MTV, living in prefab housing in the Arctic. It just does not fit with what "Eskimo" means. We are far more comfortable with snow igloos and whale blubber, harpoons and kayaks.

Although the cultures dealt with in Lucent's The Way People Live series are often historically and socially well known, the emphasis is on the personal aspects of life. Groups of people, while unquestionably affected by their politics and their governmental structures, are more than those institutions. How do people in a particular time and place educate their children? What do they eat? And how do they build their houses? What kinds of work do they do? What kinds of games do they enjoy? The answers to these questions bring these cultures to life. People's lives are revealed in the particulars and only by knowing the particulars can we understand these cultures' will to survive and their moments of weakness and greatness.

This is not to say that understanding politics does not help to understand a culture. There is no question that the Warsaw ghetto, for example, was a culture that was brought about by the politics and social ideas of Adolf

Hitler and the Third Reich. But the Jews who were crowded together in the ghetto cannot be understood by the Reich's politics. Their life was a day-to-day battle for existence, and the creativity and methods they used to prolong their lives is a vital story of human perseverance that would be denied by focusing only on the institutions of Hitler's Germany. Knowing that children as young as five or six outwitted Nazi guards on a daily basis, that Jewish policemen helped the Germans control the ghetto, that children attended secret schools in the ghetto and even earned diplomas—these are the things that reveal the fabric of life, that can inspire, intrigue, and amaze.

Books in The Way People Live series allow both the casual reader and the student to see humans as victims, heroes, and onlookers. And although humans act in ways that can fill us with feelings of sorrow and revulsion, it is important to remember that "hero," "predator," and "victim" are dangerous terms. Heaping undue pity or praise on people reduces them to objects, and strips them of their humanity.

Seeing the Jews of Warsaw only as victims is to deny their humanity. Seeing them only as they appear in surviving photos, staring at the camera with infinite sadness, is limiting, both to them and to those who want to understand them. To an object of pity, the only appropriate response becomes "Those poor creatures!" and that reduces both the quality of their struggle and the depth of their despair. No one is served by such two-dimensional views of people and their cultures.

With this in mind, The Way People Live series strives to flesh out the traditional, two-dimensional views of people in various cultures and historical circumstances. Using a wide variety of primary quotations—the words not only of the politicians and government leaders, but of the real people whose lives are being examined—each book in the series attempts to show an honest and complete picture of a culture removed from our own by time or space.

By examining cultures in this way, the reader will notice not only the glaring differences from his or her own culture, but also will be struck by the similarities. For indeed, people share common needs—warmth, good company, stability, and affirmation from others. Ultimately, seeing how people really live, or have lived, can only enrich our understanding of ourselves.

Criminals Must Be Separated from Society

For thousands of years, prisons have been used to separate criminals from law-abiding citizens. Before the eighteenth century, common penalties for criminal acts included exile, execution, and various methods of corporal punishments. Jails were viewed as temporary restrictions for antisocial behavior.

U.S. Prisons

The development of prisons in the United States began in 1817 in Auburn, New York, where prisoners were used for labor. Later, in 1870, the "probation and parole" concept moved reform measures into place. Courts began to specify minimum and maximum lengths of confinement for particular offenses.

At that time, the U.S. military owned a prison on Alcatraz Island in California's San Francisco Bay. Over many years a myriad of men were incarcerated on Alcatraz, including Civil War prisoners, Indians, Spanish-American War prisoners, and army incorrigibles. By 1911 the military had constructed the present prison building—containing about six hundred cells—which was used until 1933, when the island was sold to the Department of Justice.

During Prohibition and the Great Depression, crime and criminals in America were out of control. Because of the range of offenses, the Bureau of Pris-

The isolation of Alcatraz Island made it an ideal location for a maximum-security prison.

ons had been searching for a place to isolate the vicious, depraved inmates from the more docile ones. Alcatraz Island, surrounded by icy, treacherous waters that discouraged escape, appeared to be an ideal location for such a prison. It would be a place to segregate the "bad apples" from those prisoners who were inclined toward rehabilitation. As former inmate Jim Quillen explains in *Alcatraz from Inside*, "'Rehabilitation' was not part of the Alcatraz vocabulary, or ever considered. The institution was there for the purpose of proving to unruly prisoners that they had reached the ultimate termination of their undisciplined way of life."[1]

Alcatraz Federal Penitentiary, the most feared prison—sometimes called "Hellcatraz" and "Devil's Island of America"—was known for its lack of privileges, regimentation, and brutality. It operated from 1934 to 1963 and housed a total of 1,576 inmates (including about 30 repeat offenders) with an average of 260 criminals incarcerated at any given time. Inmates remained in the prison until they were no longer considered to be disruptive and were amenable to reform—typically eight to ten years—before being transferred to less restrictive prisons.

Public Reaction

Today Alcatraz Island is San Francisco's most popular tourist attraction. In *Progressive* magazine, Toby J. McIntosh describes the reactions of tourists who visit the prison:

> Some visitors react with shock and outrage toward the penal system. One urged continuation of the tours so that "an enraged public that is human can arise and change these zoos we call prisons." Some, on the other hand, see a visit to Alcatraz as an exercise in crime prevention. According to one letter, "I believe this will convince children that crime doesn't pay."[2]

Opinions about Alcatraz vary widely among penologists (researchers in prison management), the public, journalists, former correctional officers, adults who spent their childhoods on Alcatraz, and prisoners. They tell their stories—sometimes scary, sometimes happy, and sometimes sad—of the way people lived on Alcatraz Island during its twenty-nine years as a penitentiary.

A Tough Prison for Tough Criminals

During the 1920s and 1930s, crime in the United States appeared unmanageable. The number of people imprisoned in state and federal institutions between 1926 and 1936 rose from approximately 96,000 to 144,000. One contributing factor to the high crime rate was the passage of the Volstead Act in 1920. This law, also known as Prohibition, outlawed the manufacture and distribution of alcohol. Because it could not be obtained legally, manufacturing, selling, and transporting alcohol became profitable for criminals. Another reason for the high crime rate was the Great Depression, a time when many Americans could barely afford food, clothing, or shelter. Desperate people committed desperate acts, and a new wave of crimes—primarily kidnappings, murders, and armed robberies—took place in the decade known as "the Dirty Thirties."

Banks were prime targets of armed robbers. Those banks that remained open after the stock market crash were robbed at the rate of two a day. Bank robbers formed gangs and armed themselves with machine guns. In some instances, gangs' supplies of guns and men exceeded those of the police.

Two men rob an armored car. Armed robberies rose sharply as the Depression gripped the nation.

Furthermore, these hoodlums were made famous by their crimes. Their names and faces appeared on front pages of newspapers across the country. They enjoyed the notoriety, and their fame motivated others to commit similar violent acts. It became clear to federal law enforcement officials that something had to be done—and soon.

How to Handle a Criminal

Authorities were eager to pursue violent criminals, but arresting and jailing these high-powered gangsters created problems within the federal government's prison system. President Herbert Hoover was a Quaker and a humanitarian who believed that criminals could be reformed. "The purpose of prisons," he said, "was to restore, redeem, and reach the hearts of men—and in this light, society's needs could be more clearly seen."[3] However, something needed to be done about felons who resisted every effort at reform and presented a danger to correctional officers as well as to other prisoners.

In 1930 President Hoover established the Bureau of Prisons (BOP) within the Department of Justice. BOP was responsible for

> the safe keeping, care, protection, instruction and discipline of all persons charged with or convicted of offenses against the United States. . . . The said institution is to be planned and limited in size so as to facilitate the development of an integrated, federal penal and correctional system which will assure the proper classification and segregation of federal prisoners according to their character, the nature of their crime, their mental condition and such other factors as should be taken into consideration.[4]

J. Edgar Hoover, director of the FBI, vowed to crack down on gangsters.

In other words, those who were amenable to reform would be given the chance; for the others, a different sort of facility would be needed.

In addition to a new agency to oversee federal prisons, the government needed an effective organ to enforce federal laws. Created in 1933, the Federal Bureau of Investigation (FBI) was to be the chief law enforcement operation in the United States. The FBI was recognized as an efficient partner of local law enforcement agencies, and a campaign to curb the activities of gangsters grew naturally out of this partnership. The director of the FBI, J. Edgar Hoover, labeled the ruthless criminals as "public enemies." His primary goal was to crack down on the gang leaders who were terrifying society and put them in prison.

A Rash of Jailbreaks

However, once these gang leaders were imprisoned, their cohorts on the outside would sometimes stage daring jailbreaks to free them. In his book *Inside the Walls of Alcatraz*, former Alcatraz guard Frank Heaney describes the epidemic of jailbreaks:

> One fellow in particular, John Dillinger, had become expert at arranging escapes for his pals from Indiana State Prison. Finally he busted out of jail himself. Then Baby Face Nelson escaped, and Harvey Bailey, a companion of Machine Gun Kelly, broke out of [the state prison near] Lansing [Michigan]. Escapees were killing guards, taking hostages, and terrorizing the countryside—even Leavenworth [Federal Penitentiary in Kansas] couldn't hold them.

> The last straw was the "Kansas City Massacre." A group of criminals tried to break Frank Nash away from the FBI as they were escorting him to prison. They botched the job, killing several law enforcement officers and FBI agents, and Nash himself in the process.[5]

As Sanford Bates, director of the Bureau of Prisons, explained at the time, "The recent bold and ruthless depredations [ravaging] of a small group of desperate criminals have made the public impatient with the prisons and with crime prevention programs."[6] The need to separate unscrupulous lawbreakers from other prisoners such as first offenders, teenagers, and less hardened criminals was becoming more apparent.

The U.S. Department of Justice began searching for a site on which it could build a maximum-security prison—one that would isolate the most dangerous criminals. The prison had to be difficult to travel to and be entirely escape-proof. The strategy was to segregate the crime bosses so they could neither communicate with their gangs nor be "busted out" by their criminal friends. Remote locations in Alaska as well as in the western deserts were considered as possible sites for the new prison. The answer to the problem of locating the new prison was found in a very different place, however.

In 1932 Attorney General Homer S. Cummings, the top law enforcement official in the United States, was aboard a ship that sailed through the Golden Gate strait into the bay of San Francisco. He spied a large sign reading "U.S. Army Disciplinary Barracks" on a prison wall on Alcatraz Island. He thought this isolated place could house a federal penitentiary.

An Island Prison

As it happened, the U.S. Army was preparing to abandon the island military prison because it was too expensive to maintain. Cummings, in consultation with J. Edgar Hoover and Sanford Bates, found the disciplinary barracks ideal for a federal prison.

On October 12, 1933, ownership of Alcatraz Island was transferred from the War Department to the Department of Justice with a revocable permit. Under the terms of the permit, the Department of Justice had five years in which to prove the site's value as a federal prison. The federal prison at Alcatraz Island would be a key part of the government's campaign against predatory criminals.

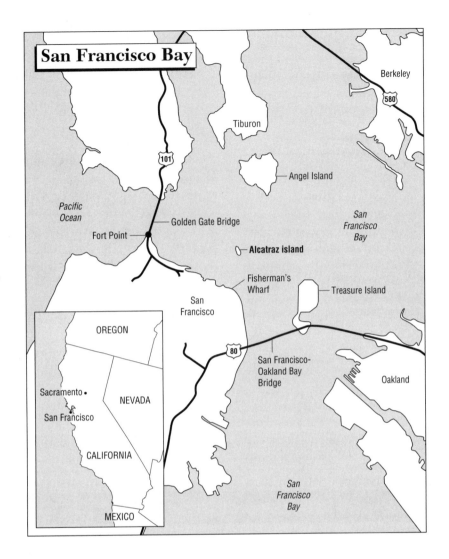

Is This Idea Logical?

Not everyone favored the new use for Alcatraz. Even though some penologists saw Alcatraz as a sensible prison for vicious and irredeemable criminals, not all employees in the correctional field agreed that such a segregated institution was either necessary or desirable. For instance, William J. Ellis of New Jersey saw "grave danger . . . of cruelties and repressive measures."[7] And Walter N. Thayer Jr. of New York believed that

"prison officials should be able to handle dangerous criminals by segregation within their own walls."[8]

The people of San Francisco were similarly unenthusiastic about the proposed new residents of the area. San Francisco citizens like Philip O'Farrell doubted that Alcatraz was escape-proof. In a 1934 letter to the editor of *Survey* magazine, O'Farrell wrote, "The old myth that escape by swimming away is impossible has recently been exploded by three girls, one of whom swam from the island to the mainland, another of whom swam from the mainland clear around the island and back to the mainland."[9]

A Plea for Tolerance

To address the concerns of San Francisco citizens about having ruthless criminals so near the city, the Department of Justice compared Alcatraz with the nearby state prison at San Quentin. The department noted that San Quentin housed fifty-five hundred inmates compared to the fewer than three hundred inmates proposed for Alcatraz. In addition, the department pledged to take every precaution, structurally and administratively, to prevent escapes. Finally, the Department of Justice tried to appeal to San Franciscans' patriotism:

> [The new prison would be] a splendid opportunity for the citizens of San Francisco to cooperate in a patriotic and public spirited manner in the Government's campaign against the criminal. The Department of Justice . . . bespeaks the cooperation and aid of this great community in the carrying on of this important and necessary activity.[10]

Alongside practical objections were some philosophical concerns. The U.S. Army's use of the island to house Confederate prisoners during the Civil War and subsequent use of the installation as a military prison troubled some people. The primitive, harsh treatment of those prisoners, who were chained in dark dungeons and were forced into hard labor, evoked images of France's notorious penal colony Devil's Island, located off the coast of French Guiana.

In response to such criticism, Attorney General Cummings said, "[Alcatraz] will not be a Devil's Island. It will be an integral part of the Federal prison system, operated in conformity with advanced ideas of penology, and with the ultimate object in view of protecting all of our communities."[11]

A Perfect Prison

In his book *On the Rock*, Alvin Karpis reveals why U.S. Attorney General Homer S. Cummings chose Alcatraz for a new federal prison. On October 12, 1933, Cummings addressed a radio audience regarding "The Recurring Problem of Crime," and he made the following announcement.

"For some time I have desired to obtain a place of confinement to which could be sent our more dangerous, intractable criminals. You can appreciate, therefore, with what pleasure I make public the fact that such a place has been found. By negotiation with the War Department we have obtained the use of Alcatraz Prison, located on a precipitous island in San Francisco Bay, more than a mile from shore. The current is swift and escapes are practically impossible. It has secure cells for 600 persons. It is in excellent condition and admirably fitted for the purpose I had in mind. Here may be isolated the criminals of the vicious and irredeemable type so that their evil influence may not be extended to other prisoners who are disposed to rehabilitate themselves."

George "Machine Gun" Kelly after being arrested in 1933. Some thought that moving all high-profile prisoners, including Kelly, to one prison was a good idea.

Differing Concepts

Alcatraz penitentiary may not have been planned as a Devil's Island, but it would be a fearful place nonetheless. FBI director J. Edgar Hoover was disgusted by the notoriety that the criminals were receiving in the newspapers, and he did not believe in criminal reform. He believed that convicts should be made to suffer for their felonies, and he used his influence to ensure that on Alcatraz they would do just that.

Hoover had a simple concept of the new penitentiary:

> Build a federal prison that would be impossible to escape from; staff it with a competent no-nonsense warden and well-trained experienced prison officers—and provide the inmates thereof with adequate food, clothing, shelter, medical care, and access to the courts.[12]

Hoover advocated no privileges and no formal attempts to rehabilitate the prisoners through formal education or job-training programs. He believed that such efforts were futile:

> There is no possibility of wiping out crime by trying to reform criminals. The house has been burned down. The tree has felt the blow of the ax, and has fallen in the forest. The house cannot be re-erected, nor the tree again point its leaves to the sky.[13]

Even within the federal prison system, there were differing opinions regarding Hoover's idea of confining all of the dangerous criminals in one so-called maximum custody–minimum privilege prison. Some officers thought it was a good idea to remove all high-profile troublemakers (Al Capone, Machine Gun Kelly, Creepy Karpis, to name

Progressive-minded James A. Johnston was selected to be Alcatraz's first warden.

a few) from their respective prison populations, where they tended to create resistance to rehabilitation programs among other inmates. However, Sanford Bates opposed the "dumping ground" concept.

James V. Bennett, assistant director of the U.S. Bureau of Prisons, stated that Bates's job as federal prison director was "to devise and manage a system of corrections that really corrects. His purpose is to help society—and to help control crime—by turning as many lawbreakers as possible into productive citizens."[14]

Combining Ideas

In an effort not to upset FBI director Hoover and his zero rehabilitation concept,

Bates and his three assistant directors compromised. Dedicated to the eventual rehabilitation of all criminals, including those on Alcatraz, Bates's program offered strong incentives for good behavior. But inmates would have to earn privileges. For example, for every forty days of good behavior, a prisoner could earn ten days off his sentence. Such "good time" would result in significant reductions in sentences. One inmate, Al Capone, for example, was a model prisoner. He served only seven years and five months of his eleven-year sentence.

This program also promised prisoners that when they earned enough good time, they could be transferred to less restrictive prisons. It succeeded with most inmates. Many became eligible and eager to transfer after four or five years at Alcatraz.

Assigning a Tough Warden

Who could carry out this demanding and contradictory mission? It would require a unique set of skills to run a prison like Alcatraz. The Department of Justice chose sixty-year-old James A. Johnston to be the first warden of Alcatraz Federal Penitentiary. Originally a banker, Johnston had been warden at California's Folsom and San Quentin prisons, two maximum-security state institutions. He had actually left the penal system and returned to banking when he was called on to be the warden on Alcatraz Island.

Johnston was known as a progressive thinker in the California criminal system. For example, as warden at Folsom State Penitentiary in 1912, he had abolished corporal punishment. During his twelve years at San Quentin, from 1913 to 1925, Johnston abolished stripes on prison clothing, established honor camps, instigated a psychological testing program, and brought in chaplains to counsel inmates. Moreover, he was committed to the idea of reforming criminals.

In 1924, a year before leaving the California penal system, Johnston had written,

If we take hate-filled, mentally warped men into prisons and do not earnestly endeavor to correct their wrong notions and replace their antisocial tendencies with finer, saner, and better ideas of their social obligations, they may leave prison worse than when they entered, [and] the prison would be a menace to society.[15]

Prison Assignments

In addition to being unusually humane for the times, Johnston was a revolutionary in other ways. In 1917, for example, Johnston obtained support from the California legislature to change the penal codes in sentencing. His plan, called the Segregation Act, changed the way prisoners were assigned to institutions. Prior to that act, a judge had the authority to assign a convicted felon to any prison—regardless of the crime committed or how the felon's behavior might affect other inmates. Now the state prison board would determine the appropriate correctional facility for each felon.

Attorney General Cummings supported the idea of controlling the placement of vicious

An Island of Many Names

Alcatraz means "pelican" in Spanish. For many centuries, the island in San Francisco Bay was inhabited mainly by birds, such as pelicans and seagulls. In 1775 Spanish explorers Juan Manuel de Ayala and Jose Canizores charted and named the piece of land La Isla de Los Alcatraces, or "the Island of Pelicans."

In 1827 Captain Frederick Beechey, a British officer, made a second survey of San Francisco Bay. He changed the spelling to "Alcatrasses."

Many misspellings and name changes followed. During the American Civil War, the island had a variety of names, including Alcatraces, Alcatrasses, Alcatrazes, and Alcatrasas. Americans, who came to California after the 1848 gold discovery, called the small isle Bird Island or White Island.

criminals: "It is of fundamental importance that prisoners be properly classified and segregated."[16] Decades later, the warden's plan would continue to be responsible for determining the prison population on Alcatraz.

Committed to Alcatraz

After carefully reviewing records of inmates in the federal prison system, the most uncooperative gangsters, killers, and kidnappers were chosen to be transferred to Alcatraz. At the maximum-security prison, prisoners could expect toughness, but also fairness, from the experienced Warden Johnston.

Once a prisoner had been committed to Alcatraz, he was totally at the mercy of the warden and his staff. Johnston had promised the Department of Justice that the confirmed criminals of Alcatraz would not be coddled:

Insistence on absolute obedience to regulations and the orders of those in authority is essential. I would not make a fetish [ob-

session] of rules. I prefer reason. But there are rules of reason and reasonable rules, and prisoners should be compelled to obey them; otherwise no progress can be made toward reformation, because chief of the criminal's faults is disobedience.[17]

Johnston recognized, however, that some prisoners would resist all efforts at reform. The new warden described the difference between professional, hardened criminals and those who wanted to improve themselves:

When a man is known to have committed a dozen or more serious crimes and to have been properly convicted and imprisoned three or four times, it would seem as if he had demonstrated unwillingness or inability to earn a living honestly and to respect the rights of others.[18]

During the fourteen years that Johnston served as warden, his administrative policies were respected. The following facts validated his success as a warden: "Not one prisoner has

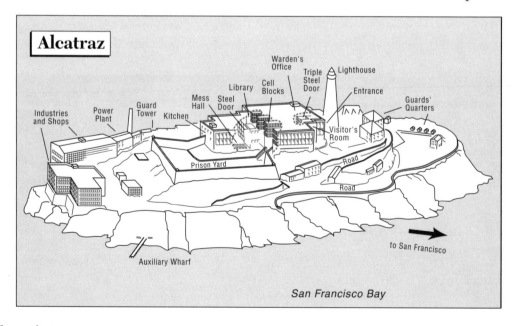

Fierce winds and thick fogs in San Francisco Bay made piloting ships difficult. Author Marilyn Tower Oliver discusses the building of lighthouses on Alcatraz Island in her book *Alcatraz Prison in American History*. The first lighthouse beam could be seen by ships fourteen miles out to sea.

"To help ships navigate through the foggy bay, the [first] lighthouse [built in 1854] had

Alcatraz's first lighthouse, built in 1854.

a fog bell that weighed a thousand pounds. It took one man forty-five minutes to wind up the bell. After it was wound, the bell would ring six times a minute, once every ten seconds. The sounds would last for five hours. Then the bell would have to be rewound. [Moaning foghorns replaced the bells and recently tone generators upgraded the system.]

In 1909, when the army built a prison cell house, the new building blocked the light from the lighthouse. The army decided to tear down the old lighthouse and build a new one. That lighthouse is still in use. The only time it was dark was on June 2, 1970, when a fire broke out. The light has been replaced several times. The earliest light was fueled by whale oil. Later, kerosene was used. Today, the light is electric [and automated]. The Alcatraz lighthouse is the oldest continually operating lighthouse on the West Coast."

escaped alive, so far as known; only one prisoner committed suicide from 1934 to 1948; fewer prisoners become psychotic in this prison than in other Federal prisons."[19]

A New Federal Prison

Because Johnston was the first warden at Alcatraz, he participated in its intricate remodeling plans. Besides housing six hundred single cells, the property also had a medical facility, mess hall, kitchen, library, barbershop, workshops, laundry building, and an exercise yard.

As the facility's new owner, the Department of Justice prepared to make many

physical changes to the twenty-year-old concrete building on the top of the hill. They spent $263,000 to convert the U.S. Army Disciplinary Barracks, Pacific Branch, into the U.S. Penitentiary, Alcatraz Island, California.

This penitentiary for America's most dangerous criminals was designed to be escape-proof. Substantial changes to the facility itself were needed to make this aim a reality.

Improvements

Advanced security devices included replacing the soft-iron flat bars with uncuttable steel round bars on 336 cells and on all windows.

New locking devices and two gun galleries completed the safeguard plans to the cell house. Electronic metal detectors were installed at the dock and at the entrance to the cell house to detect hidden guns or knives on both prisoners and visitors.

Other preparations included installing searchlight towers and floodlights; communication devices, such as shortwave radios and telephones to the mainland; and tear-gas outlets in the mess hall ceiling and main entrance. All of these safety features served to maintain protection against and during riots.

Four new guard towers were added to allow a bird's-eye view of the twelve-acre island and its activities. A new armory for weapons, enclosed in steel walls, was constructed near the main entrance. The complete compound of prison buildings, covering seven acres, was wrapped in barbed wire.

The mile and a quarter of numbing forty-eight-degree Fahrenheit waters that separated the prison from the city of San Francisco provided a formidable barrier in preventing escape from the island, but the federal authorities took no chances. Coast Guard and prison boats policed the waters, ready to pick up any swimming escapee.

Authorities even took into account the possibility that someone might try to pick up an escaping prisoner in a boat. Signs posted around the perimeter of the island warned boats to stay two hundred yards away from the island. Buoys marked the distance, and if vessels violated the rule, guards opened fire on them.

Other Staff at Alcatraz

The warden knew Alcatraz would have to accommodate more than just the inmates. It would be practical for correction officers to live on the island as well. In addition to the prison facilities, Johnston ordered the barracks buildings altered to provide quarters for single men and a small number of families. He wanted to make sure that custodial officers would be available, even when off duty, to meet any emergency.

When Alcatraz first opened, there were approximately seventy-five employees. About fifty were correctional officers, or guards, who transferred from other institutions. Unlike other prisons, which had a usual ratio of one guard for every seven inmates, Alcatraz was unique: There was one guard for every three inmates.

Other employees included a member of the Coast Guard, a lighthouse keeper, Public Health Service staff, a doctor, a medical technician, civilian workers who were foremen in the industries, and administrative personnel. In August 1934, with the remodeling completed and the staff in place, the U.S. Penitentiary on Alcatraz Island was ready for its first tenants.

Arriving on the Rock: A Life Like No Other

When the military prison run by the U.S. Army closed in 1933, thirty-two convicts remained at Alcatraz. These convicts helped remodel the cells for the first inmate transfers. In August of the following year, the Bureau of Prisons relocated the nation's worst criminals to Alcatraz.

Journalist Edwin H. Sutherland writes in the September 10, 1949, issue of the *Saturday Review of Literature*, "One or more of three criteria is used in the selection of prisoners for confinement in Alcatraz Island Prison—the number and violence of previous crimes, the number of escapes from prisons, and the extent to which the criminal is a trouble-maker."[20]

"The Rock," as the prison was called, was considered the ultimate sentence before death by execution. In the November 2, 1935, *Saturday Evening Post*, Frederick R. Bechdolt gives another explanation of how prisoners were selected to go to Alcatraz:

No man is sentenced to the place. When the warden of a Federal penitentiary finds a prisoner to be a source of trouble or a danger—the man may be a smuggler of drugs; he may be plotting a break; perhaps his outside connections are breeding disturbance within the walls—the case is reported to the Federal Prison Bureau. If the bureau so decides, the convict is transferred to Alcatraz.[21]

Criminals transferred to the Rock had shown themselves to be tough, violent, calcu-

lating, and hardened. Author Howard Needham describes the convicts: "They were rejects from society's rejected. Alcatraz was their last stopping place. All were lifers or long-termers. Many had shown that they could kill while trying to escape."[22]

The Long Train Ride From Leavenworth

Trains, buses, and boats transported prisoners to Alcatraz. Alvin Karpis, labeled "Public Enemy Number One" by FBI director J. Edgar Hoover, was incarcerated at Leavenworth Federal Prison in Kansas. In his book, *On the Rock*, Karpis describes how he was transferred to Alcatraz in August 1936:

"Put all the belongings you want to keep in this pillow case Karpis—you and a lot of other guys are leaving tonight for Alcatraz," I'm told by the screw [guard]. "Come out in just your shorts." We stop in front of Dimmenza's cell and the screw shouts, "You too. . . ." We're taken to a wing of the administration building where we are the last to arrive. The room is filled with cons putting on clothing from paper bags; only two bags remained unopened—one for me and one for Phil Dimmenza. In the bag is a pair of pants, a shirt, a pair of sneakers, a comb, a handkerchief, a toothbrush, and a coat. . . .

Alvin "Creepy" Karpis

Alvin "Creepy" Karpis, one of Alcatraz's most notorious inmates.

Karpis served twenty-six years at Alcatraz, the longest term of any prisoner, beginning in 1936. His crimes included shooting a Kansas policeman, bank robberies, and two notable kidnappings, both in St. Paul, Min-

nesota, in 1934. Families of the kidnap victims paid Karpis and his gang hefty ransoms. In the case of brewery millionaire William Hamm Jr., the gang collected over one hundred thousand dollars. When Karpis kidnapped Edward Bremmer, the president of a Minnesota bank, he collected a two-hundred-thousand-dollar ransom—all in marked bills. The bills were quickly traced to a home in New Orleans, where he was arrested. Karpis, who had eight career aliases, was particularly proud of one trick he used to avoid being caught by law enforcement officials. He explains the trick in his book *On the Rock*

"I removed [my finger] prints when I was on the outside. Doc Moran had first cut the circulation to each finger then shot my finger tips full of cocaine before taking a scalpel and shaving all the layers of skin off each finger, much as you would sharpen a pencil. The operation was a success, my fingerprints never returned. The idea was not to prevent my identification if caught, but to prevent my capture by not leaving a trail of tell-tale prints in every hotel room and automobile."

In 1962, officials transferred Karpis from Alcatraz to McNeil Island federal prison, and then paroled him to his home in Canada. It has been said that he committed suicide in Spain in 1979.

Twenty of us line up, double file, shackled by an ankle to the guy beside us, handcuffed individually, and march out of the building onto a railroad car inside the prison walls. The windows of the train are screened and barred; about three feet in-

side the car at each end is a barred door. Outside each door sits a screw with a twelve-gauge riot gun. Once we are inside our jail on wheels, it begins to roll. The large back gate of the prison opens to allow the prison switch engine to pull us out and onto another railroad track where a regular switch engine waits. At Lawrence, Kansas, our prison car is attached to the back of the Overland Limited, a crack train of the Union Pacific, which carries us to the Coast.[23]

As usual, these twenty inmates were transferred under secrecy. The well-guarded train traveled three days and included stops at Topeka, Kansas; Denver, Colorado; Cheyenne, Wyoming; and Ogden, Utah. At each stop, Department of Justice men lined up on both sides of the coaches and allowed no one to come within fifty feet.

The long trip ended at a dock in Richmond, California. The smell of saltwater drifted into the prison car. At this point, the railroad car would switch tracks onto a long pier extending into San Francisco Bay. The guards would hustle the prisoners from the train and order them to climb down a steep fifteen-foot iron-rung

ladder into a boat. Karpis describes the climb down: "We descend carefully, two at a time, my 128-pound body shackled to the 200-pound Italian who was my neighbour in isolation. 'Jesus,' I think, 'I hope this [guy] doesn't slip or we'll go down like the Titanic!'"[24]

Prisoners From McNeil Island

Other prisoners transferred to Alcatraz from McNeil Island, a federal penitentiary located several miles off the coast of Washington State in Puget Sound. All federal prisoners from the states of California, Arizona, Nevada, Washington, and Utah were incarcerated at McNeil. In his autobiography *Last Train to Alcatraz*, written in the third person, Leon "Whitey" Thompson describes his transfer out of McNeil to Alcatraz in 1958. On the morning of his transfer, he is awakened at 5:00 A.M. by a guard:

The first load of federal prisoners, transported in a sealed train car, arrives at Alcatraz on August 22, 1934.

"Okay Thompson, up and out of there," he ordered. Whitey slowly moved out from under the blanket, and as he did so, he heard the padlock being removed from the cell door. He slid his feet over the edge of the bunk, and placed them on the cold concrete floor. His eyes were not yet accustomed to the darkness of the cell, and he couldn't see a thing as he fumbled for his clothes.

The guard yelled at him, "Never mind your clothes. Don't touch anything, just come out of there the way you are."[25]

Thompson's experience was typical. The prisoners were cold and shivering. Two guards, one in front, the other behind, escorted each inmate to the shower room. After showering, guards strip-searched their charge, and ordered him to shave his beard. Guards handcuffed each of the six prisoners. Next,

they attached shackles, or ankle irons, and linked the six men to each other with chains. The chains allowed only twelve-inch steps. If the men got out of step, the irons cut into their ankles, leaving them raw and swollen.

They shuffled through several doors and gates that unlocked in front of them and re-locked after they had passed through. Finally they reached the dock where the prisoners and their three guards boarded the prison boat.

The boat took them to Steilacoom, a whistle-stop city near Tacoma, Washington. There they boarded the Canadian Pacific train, which was loaded with tourists—most of them headed for San Francisco. The Federal Bureau of Prisons had reserved a special compartment for the men. Two guards remained inside the locked compartment with the prisoners while one guard stayed outside the door.

Handcuffed to a restraining belt and shackled and chained, the men found it diffi-

The boat officer casts off as the Warden Johnston prison ferry leaves for Alcatraz Island. The boat was used to transport prisoners to the island.

With its cold, imposing mass rising sharply out of the water, Alcatraz resembled a battleship to some people.

cult to eat, use the toilet, wash their hands, smoke, or sit comfortably. The six prisoners made it tough for the guards to keep order. The chained men cussed, fought, and tangled with each other throughout the trip.

During the train ride, a parade of curious tourists peeked into the compartment to get a look at the shackled prisoners. In Oakland, California, the prisoners exited the train under the watchful eyes of a dozen city policemen who lined the platform. A bus with two Alcatraz guards snaked its way through traffic to the Oakland Bay Bridge, then to the Fort Mason dock. The *Warden Johnston* prison ferryboat shuttled the nine passengers across the bay to Alcatraz.

Alcatraz

As the San Francisco skyline receded, the cliffs and stark forbidding concrete buildings of Alcatraz loomed ahead. The first glimpse of Alcatraz would likely have filled even the most hardened convict with dread.

Because of its terraces and buildings, some people thought the island resembled an enormous battleship. Jutting one hundred and eighty feet at its highest point, the island was primarily composed of bare stone, gray concrete, and tool-proof steel. It measured around seven hundred yards from end to end.

The bare rock rising out of the San Francisco Bay had few trees and little vegetation.

Armed personnel stood guard on the catwalk connecting the guard tower to the adjoining building as new prisoners arrived on the island.

The area was prone to fog, damp winds, and cold, even in summer. In June and July, guards sometimes wore overcoats. As prisoners approached the island, they saw a huge sign posted on a brick wall:

UNITED STATES
PENITENTIARY
ALCATRAZ ISLAND AREA 12 ACRES
1 1/2 MILES TO TRANSPORT DOCK
ONLY GOVERNMENT BOATS PERMITTED
OTHERS MUST KEEP OFF 200 YARDS
NO ONE ALLOWED ASHORE
WITHOUT A PASS[26]

Unfriendly Greeters

At the island dock, each sweaty, exhausted prisoner was greeted by a line of armed guards on the catwalk that joined a three-story building and a gun tower on steel stilts near the water edge. Karpis describes his experience at the Alcatraz dock, where a six-foot-tall official in a brass-buttoned blue uniform decorated with five stars and four bars of gold cloth screamed at the new inmates:

Take a good look! . . . Them guns you see aimed at you ain't nothin' to what we can come up with. Remember this, if any of you . . . start thinkin' of gettin' away from here. You're sent here 'cause they're afraid of you in them other prisons, but we ain't![27]

The new inmates shuffled into two trucks and were driven up the long, twisting road to the top of the rocky island. Stopping at a barred gate, the drivers signaled a guard in a tower more than a quarter of a mile away. In response, the guard telephoned the warden, then pulled a lever that opened the gate.

The trucks moved through the gate and stopped. The prisoners slid off the trucks' benches and into a narrow hallway where a guard unlocked and removed the sixteen pounds of metal shackles and irons from their swollen ankles.

Next, the new prisoners emptied their pockets and passed through a metal detector booth. A buzzer or light instantly alerted guards if an inmate had hidden metal objects, such as a knife or gun, on himself. Inside the booth, an officer watched a device with a telltale needle that would reveal small bits of hidden steel or iron. A 1935 *Saturday Evening Post* article describes one incident:

> [A] convict [known for smuggling contraband] finished emptying his pockets. "I'm clean," he said. . . . The guard in the booth did not shift his eyes from the object overhead. "This fellow has still got a batting average," he announced. Then the guard outside began searching. He explored pockets, shoes, seams and hair. At last he thrust a pair of tweezers into the prisoner's ear and brought out a short piece of watch spring wrapped in brown cigarette paper. His companion looked down for the first time and nodded. "All right. Pass on."[28]

Consequently, inmates called the metal detector booths "mechanical stool pigeons" and "snitch boxes." The moveable booths, which were placed throughout the prison area, became a constant irritant in a prisoner's life.

First Entry

The next admitting procedure for new inmates included showers and strip searches,

Inmates returning to the cell house from the recreation yard pass through a metal detector. The prisoners called the metal detectors "mechanical stool pigeons" or "snitch boxes."

Both visitors and inmates had to comply with visitation rules.

the first step in deflating egos. "I never saw a naked man yet," Warden Johnston later said, "who could maintain any sort of dignity."[29]

Issuance of prison uniforms followed. Early uniforms were one-piece coveralls. Later they changed to denim shirts and pants, a belt, and issue shoes. Each prisoner was assigned a number representing the numeric order of his entry into the prison, preceded by the letters *AZ* (for *Alcatraz*). The numbers, stamped on three-inch by eight-inch duck cloth, a durable cotton fabric, were later sewn on the front and the back of the uniform.

Fingerprints and facial photographs followed. Photos of inmates—left and right profiles and a front view—recorded them as official residents of the Rock. The front view displayed a four-by-seven-inch identification plate which included two sets of numbers: the

inmates identification number and the date of his admission to the prison. Whitey Thompson's nameplate read,

U.S. PENITENTIARY
ALCATRAZ
1465
7 19 58[30]

Warden Johnston had a standard speech for the new group of prisoners: "You are entitled to food, clothing, shelter and medical attention. Anything else you get is a privilege."[31] Prisoner Karpis later recalled the instructions that followed when he entered in 1936:

We have a silent system here! At no time are you to talk or make a noise while in the cell house or mess hall at Alcatraz!

You convicts are now going to the dining room to eat. When you finish eating, put your silverware on your food tray and sit with your arms folded across your chest until you are ordered to leave.

Take as much or as little as you wish to eat but finish everything on your plate. If you fail to eat everything you take, you will end up in the hole eating bread and water once a day. . . . A book of rules is in your cell.[32]

The Book of Rules

The 1956 revised edition of the *Institution Rules and Regulations* for inmates of Alcatraz had nineteen typewritten pages listing fifty-three rules. The first rule spelled out the warden's expectations:

Leon "Whitey" Thompson was an inmate at Alcatraz from 1958 to 1962. He transferred there from the federal penitentiary on McNeil Island, where he had already served ten years of his fifteen-year sentence.

Thompson never knew his mother and was one of seven children growing up in New Haven, Connecticut. He carried emotional scars from an abusive, drunken father. The boy had been rejected by schoolmates as well as adults. As a result, he hated and distrusted most people. Thompson began his career of crime at age thirteen by robbing a country grocery store. He continued to commit armed robberies for the next twelve years, until authorities arrested him and sentenced him to McNeil Island.

Thompson had a hair-trigger temper and was extremely dangerous when provoked. Because of his foul, offensive language and raging temper, Thompson spent forty-two days in "segregation" at McNeil and forfeited over six hundred days of good time.

At Alcatraz, Thompson developed friendships for the first time in his life. Oil painting in prison helped him gain self-esteem and acceptance. Slowly he emerged from the shell that had engulfed him for many years. Unfortunately, after Thompson's release from Alcatraz, his prison stints continued for another twelve years before he turned his life around.

Thompson now lives in northern California with his wife and dogs. He works with young offenders at the California Youth Authority, speaks to teenagers in schools, and lectures at prison prerelease programs. Thompson also autographs his continuing autobiographies *Last Train to Alcatraz* and *Alcatraz Merry-Go-Round* for tourists at Alcatraz.

Ex-inmate Leon Thompson talks with young visitors to Alcatraz.

Al "Scarface" Capone

Al Capone was among the prisoners who arrived at Alcatraz the first year it opened in 1934. Because Capone's left cheek had been slashed by a small-time hoodlum, people nicknamed him "Scarface." In spite of the fact that Capone's mother was devoutly religious and his father was a respectable barber, all of their children grew up to be criminals.

As leader of the Italian Mafia, Capone controlled Chicago with machine guns. His organization took in $120 million a year from bootlegging, prostitution, and gambling. Even though Capone had four arrests, he seemed untouchable by the law. Witnesses became silent; no one would testify or serve on a jury. The charge that finally landed Capone in prison was twenty-two counts of federal income tax evasion. Capone began his eleven-year sentence at the federal prison in Atlanta, but authorities soon transferred him to Alcatraz.

Other inmates detested Capone because of his wealth, short sentence, and because his men had "taken care of" some of their friends. Fearing for his life, Capone did not use the recreation yard; instead, he retreated to a basement shower room where he played his banjo. His jobs at Alcatraz included laundry work and mopping the shower room and latrine. In less than five years, doctors diagnosed Capone with irre-

Chicago mob boss Al Capone was one of Alcatraz's first prisoners.

versible syphilis. When they transferred him to The Terminal Island Prison hospital in southern California, the former mobster was confused, babbling, and docile. After his release, Capone died in his Florida estate in 1947 at the age of forty-eight.

Good Conduct means conducting yourself in a quiet and orderly manner and keeping your cell neat, clean and free from contraband [nonapproved goods]. It means obeying the rules of the Institution and displaying a co-operative attitude. It also means obeying orders of Officials, Officers and other employees without delay or argument."[33]

Another rule spelled out regulations regarding money. Money was forbidden. Unlike most prisons, Alcatraz did not have a commissary from which to make incidental purchases such as cigarettes, candy, and name-brand items. An inmate's earnings from industrial jobs within the prison were deposited in the Prisoner's Trust Fund. This fund operated like a savings account in a bank, except without accumulated interest. With the associate warden's approval, an inmate could authorize withdrawal of funds to pay attorney's fees, to purchase textbooks and educational materials, and to give money to dependents.

Clothing Restrictions

The regulation booklet listed additional clothing restrictions. Inmates were to wear the standard uniform for all normal activities inside the cell house, such as visits, interviews, meals, and movies.

Regulations required shirts to be buttoned, except for the top collar button and sleeve cuffs rolled down and buttoned. Inmates wore the uniform to and from work and in the recreation yard. However, a cap, coat, or raincoat could be added. Other issued clothing included a bathrobe and slippers (to be worn when going to and from the bath), three pairs of socks, one pair of tennis shoes (to be worn only in the recreation yard), one light undershirt, one pair of boxer shorts, and two handkerchiefs.

The regulation book also stated, "Special work clothing is issued for work details. This special clothing will be kept at the place of work and will not be brought to the Yard or cell house."[34] Culinary, or kitchen workers, barbers, and orderlies, hospital or officer attendants, dressed in white shirts and sometimes white pants. Only the culinary workers kept their uniforms in their cells and wore them en route between their cell and the culinary unit. Because they handled food, culinary workers showered on Mondays, Wednesdays, and Fridays. However, most inmates showered only twice a week, on Tuesdays and Saturdays, and received fresh clothing at that time. Once a week, inmates exchanged soiled sheets, pillowcases, and towels for clean linens.

Quarantine

A new inmate was put into a quarantine unit in C Block for up to thirty days until he was assigned a job. During this time, a committee of officials interviewed the new inmate. Officials such as the warden, the associate warden, the guard captain, the chaplain, a counselor, and a foreman from industries familiarized themselves with the prisoner's background. They told the inmate about the jobs available, and quizzed him about his desires and qualifications. Frank Heaney describes the available work assignments for the new inmates:

> During that first month, if they wanted to work (work was a privilege), they might be allowed to sweep inside the cell house. Or they might be what they'd call a yardbird, down in the exercise yard, cleaning up after the people were out of there. He might do other types of somewhat menial work, eventually waiting for an opening in the industries. Other inmates could transfer around, and usually had priority, so it generally took some time before there was an opening.[35]

A First Evaluation

In the case of inmate Whitey Thompson, a classification counselor came to his cell on his second day. The counselor assessed the newcomer's abilities and probable behavior patterns. In addition, he approved requests

New prisoners were quarantined in C Block for up to thirty days while they were interviewed and assessed for work assignments.

for visitors and correspondence. The classification counselor said to Thompson,

> Ordinarily there is a three-month waiting period here on Alcatraz before a newcomer can have a visit. In your case you don't have to wait the three-month period, and we're allowing you two visits a month. They cannot be a former inmate, do you have two people for your list, like members of your immediate family? [Thompson answered,] I don't want no visits nor do I want to write to anyone.[36]

Because officials used the cancellation of visits and correspondence as a form of discipline, they found this type of response discouraging. The counselor told Thompson

that they had job openings in the glove shop and the kitchen. Thompson chose the glove shop. At the end of the interview, the counselor told Thompson that he would be moved to a new cell that afternoon.

After the noon count cleared and the work call sounded, the guard lieutenant, carrying a clipboard, called off the names of Thompson and the five other new prisoners from McNeil Island. "You men are going to make a cell move. I want you to walk around B and C Block to find an empty cell of your choice. Then report immediately to the Cell House desk, and give me the cell number."[37] Early prisoners did not have a choice of cells.

During the twenty-nine years that Alcatraz was a federal prison, over fifteen hundred men lived in the cell house. Different cell blocks and cells served different purposes.

The Cell House

Inmates lived in the huge cell house at the top of the hill. The brick and steel building contained four cell blocks: A, B, C, and D. Each cell block was three tiers high, with individual cells. The two inside cell blocks, B and C, contained a total of 336 cells. Only cell blocks B and C had been initially remodeled with tool-proof steel bars and modern locking devices, allowing designated cell doors to roll open individually or as a group. Plastered cement walls separated the cells.

A thirty-inch-wide utility corridor ran the length and height of each cell block. This middle tunnel was cluttered with sewer and water pipes and electrical wires. Barred and wire-meshed gun galleries were located at both ends of the cell blocks. Armed officers had a view of every cell from the multilevel gun galleries.

Inmates named the cell house corridors. "Times Square" was in front of the dining room. "Broadway" was the main corridor that separated B Block from C Block. The outer, narrower corridor of blocks A and B was dubbed "Michigan Boulevard," and C and D aisle was "Seedy Street." This gray-green cell

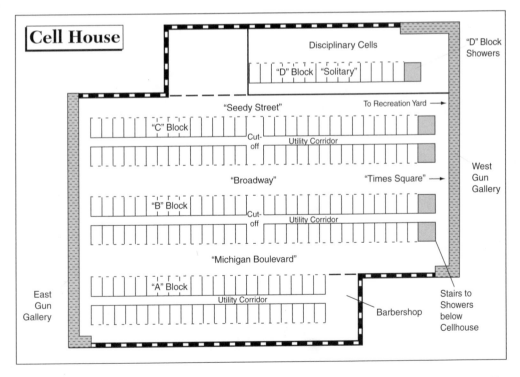

Cell House

Disciplinary Cells

"D" Block Showers

"D" Block   "Solitary"

"Seedy Street"

To Recreation Yard →

"C" Block

Cut-off

Utility Corridor

West Gun Gallery

"Broadway"

"Times Square" →

"B" Block

Cut-off

Utility Corridor

"Michigan Boulevard"

East Gun Gallery

"A" Block

Utility Corridor

Barbershop

Stairs to Showers below Cellhouse

house had shiny polished cement floors and smelled of disinfectant.

Home for a Long Time

Prisoner Alvin Karpis described the cell he occupied at Alcatraz in 1936:

> It is eight feet by five and one-half feet with an eight-foot ceiling on which is mounted a twenty-watt light bulb. The bunk is made up for me with two white sheets and a blanket as well as two more blankets folded military style across the foot of the bed. The bunk hangs by chains from the wall and folds up against the wall when necessary. The mattress and pillow are cotton. The toilet is at the end of the bunk beside a small wash basin in the center of the back wall. Under the basin a heavy mesh screen a foot off the floor encloses a ventilator eight inches wide and six inches high. Eighteen inches from the

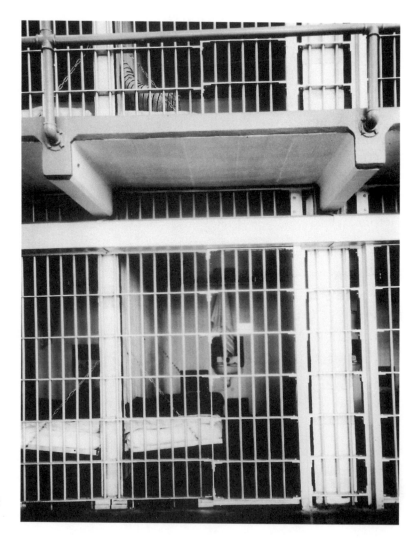

A bank of eight-foot-by-five-and-a-half-foot cells, where prisoners spent most of their day.

ceiling a shelf of one-inch plank, one foot wide, sits against the back wall supported by three metal pegs, one in the center of the back wall and one from each side wall of the cell. On the shelf I find the following items: a safety razor, an aluminum cup for drinking water, a second one with a cake of Williams shaving soap in it, a shaving brush, a mirror made of highly polished metal, a toothbrush, a container full of toothpowder, a bar of playmate soap, a comb, a pair of nail clippers, a sack of Stud smoking tobacco, a corncob pipe, a roll of toilet paper, a can of brown shoe polish, a green celluloid eye shade, a whisk broom for sweeping out the cell, and the rule book we were told to read. In the middle of the wall, opposite the bed, a steel table and seat fold against the wall when not in use. On the underside of the long shelf are several clothes hooks.[38]

D Block, photographed here on June 1, 1941, after its remodeling.

Karpis had no idea that he would occupy this same cell for nearly twenty-six years. He had the distinction of being the longest incarcerated inmate at Alcatraz.

D Block: Solitary

Life in the cell block was never easy, but misbehavior made life even more difficult. A special area was used for discipline. For the first seven years, officials isolated vicious inmates in the pitch-black underground dungeons. Alvin Karpis tells of the time that he spent in the dungeon in 1936:

I'm escorted down the steep steps leaving daylight, humanity, and civilization above. Flashlights jerk roughly across ancient slabs of stone cut by primitive Spanish instruments in another century.

Somewhere in the depths of the rocky island, the granite expression on the [guard's] face is momentarily illuminated in the beam from his flashlight as he clumsily chains and padlocks the door shut. A moment later, I'm alone in the darkness. Water is running off the walls, continuously, keeping the dungeon cell damp. There is no toilet. At noon I receive two slices of bread which is the only meal of the day. One of my greatest fears during the three days in the barren tunnels is that I'll fall asleep and wake up, my body covered with large rats whose green eyes sparkle from jagged recesses.[39]

Because the two outer cell blocks, A and D, had not been remodeled, they were not in regular use, except to isolate a few troublemakers. However, by 1941 Alcatraz had rebuilt the bars on D Block cells and opened them up as disciplinary cells. Former inmate Jim Quillen describes D Block in his book *Alcatraz from Inside*:

> All the cells on D block had steel walls, ceilings and floors, as well as special tool-resistant barred fronts. Most of the cells in D block were larger and better lighted than those in the main cell house, and

The most troublesome inmates were sent to the dark, empty strip cell.

faced the outer wall of the building. This had advantages as well as disadvantages. From some of the cells on the upper tier, the view was beautiful, but in the wet, windy, foggy weather the windows were a curse because of the cold they allowed in, making it miserable for everyone.[40]

Forty-two cells—all with steel bars, floors, walls, and ceilings—made up D Block. It was also known as the treatment unit(TU), for its use as the place where prison officials dealt with problem inmates. Thirty-six were isolation cells with barred fronts. The other six were solitary cells, one of which was a strip cell. Prisoners called solitary "the hole" because the cubicles had a two-hundred-pound steel door blocking out all light. For some inmates, being in solitary was a macho trip—it proved that they were tough. The strip cell was the ultimate punishment. It had no toilet or basin—just a hole in the floor for bathroom purposes. Sometimes the inmate was left naked in this dark cell. Incarceration in the strip cell usually lasted for only a couple of days.

Experiencing the Strip Cell

However, that was not the case for inmate Alvin Karpis. In 1952 Karpis was accused (wrongly, according to him) of being the ringleader in a riot. He spent twenty-two days in the strip cell. Karpis later described the experience:

> The double doors block out all light even in the middle of the day. The walls and floors are steel, nothing else exists in the small cupboard-like space except a hole in the floor which is the toilet. A guard flushes it from outside the cell. Otherwise, nothing. No bed, no blanket, no book, no shelf, no sink—nothing but

Solitary Leads Some Inmates to Self-Destruction

In *Escape from Alcatraz*, author J. Campbell Bruce tells a gruesome tale about how one inmate in solitary confinement, John Stadig, finally left the prison system.

"A guard handed in lunch one day and then, instead of standing watch, let Stadig alone behind the locked, solid door. Stadig bent a prong of the fork and jabbed it in his wrist, worked it under the big vein and pried the vein out into the open. Then he bit it in two. He was prying the vein out of the other wrist when the guard returned for the luncheon tray. Besides his wrist, Stadig punctured a hole in the concept of Alcatraz as a super-lockup for troublemakers: too much of a trouble on The Rock, he was shipped back to Leavenworth. The day he arrived there, safely locked away in a cell, he broke a lens of his eyeglasses, took a jagged piece and sliced his jugular vein. He had at last found release."

the pathetic initials and dates scratched on the walls by former occupants.

Standing naked on the damp steel floor, I hear the doors lock behind me and realize that if I had the ability to raise my infected arm as well as my healthy one to my side, I would touch both walls and that I might walk about three steps before colliding against the wall at the end of the cell.

I am supposed to receive one subsistence meal a day. The bread and water diet has been replaced by a dixie cup of mush . . . [mashed] leftovers from the main line—beets, carrots, spinach . . . a sickly looking puke that is more liquid than solid. . . . Days seem like nights and nights seem like days. At intervals sunlight floods into my eyes leaving me blinded as I grope for the dixie cup and force myself to swallow half the contents.[41]

Change Your Attitude—or Else

The next grade up from the strip cell was the five solitary cells, called "black holes." According to Quillen, "Confinement in the hole could be for any reason: intoxication, fighting, assaulting an officer, stealing food, destruction of government property, escape attempts or possession of contraband of any nature."[42]

The solitary cells were equipped with a toilet and basin, and inmates were given a mattress, pillow, and blanket after supper. Two cell doors—one, a two-hundred-pound steel door that sealed off all light, day and night; the other, a barred door—kept the inmates aware of their punishment. The solitary confinement cell doors were both electronically and key operated. The outer solid steel door had to be unlocked electronically from the gun gallery, and the inner barred door required a key that was lowered by the gun gallery officer. Officials used these cells as a means of changing a prisoner's attitude.

Guard Frank Heaney said, "Typical bad attitude would be shown by spitting on us, throwing food, urine or feces at us, cursing us. I've had all that thrown at me at one time or another."[43]

If the inmate's attitude did not improve, he remained in the hole—sometimes as long as nineteen consecutive days, which was the maximum time an inmate could be confined in solitary. However, if at the end of the maximum time period the inmate continued to cause problems, guards removed him, fed him a full meal, allowed him to brush his teeth, and then returned him to the hole for another nineteen days.

A "Solitary" Experience

Assigned to work in the kitchen, Jim Quillen, along with three other culinary workers, spent several months plotting an escape through a basement floor tunnel. However, someone "ratted" about the plan, either to the authorities or to another inmate, and two of the men were charged with attempted escape. For this, they served nineteen days in the black hole, followed by indefinite segregation in D Block.

Quillen later said, "A day in the hole was like an eternity."[44] In the hole, inmates saw no light except during meals. Officers flicked lights on at 6:30 A.M. and passed breakfast through a slot inside the barred door. The unappetizing meal came in one big lump. Oatmeal and prunes soaked into bread. The meal did not include milk or sugar. Inmates knew to dump the food down the toilet if they could not eat it—otherwise officers would withhold their next meal. The prisoner, hopeful that the next meal would be better, did not want that to happen. After twenty minutes, inmates had to roll up their mattress, pillow, and blanket and set them in the three-foot space that separated the inner and outer doors. Then officers flicked out the lights until the next meal.

While in the hole, inmates wore only boxer shorts, socks, and coveralls. Because the steel walls and floor of the cell retained the cold, inmates felt chilled most of the time. The coldness, isolation, and darkness forced Quillen to do something to keep his mind occupied:

I invented a game simply to retain my sanity. I would tear a button from my coveralls, then fling it into the air, turn around in circles several times and, with my eyes closed, get on the floor on my hands and knees and search for the button. When it was found, I would repeat the entire routine over and over until I was exhausted, or my knees were so sore I could not continue.[45]

The button game, together with cell pacing, also helped Quillen to keep warm.

D Block: Isolation

The thirty-six isolation cells had tool-proof steel bars but were slightly larger than cells in B and C Blocks. Quillen explains isolation:

Confinement in D block would be for a matter of one month to years! The only privilege allowed in this block was reading. You were locked in your cell twenty-four hours each day. Meals and all activity, except for a weekly bath, were in your cell. Talking was permitted to those who were housed in cells next to yours, but in a moderate tone only. Inmates were, by law, allowed a period of recreation in the prison yard, but this was never enforced for the D block's population.[46]

Those inmates in the upper tier were usually in isolation for long terms. Typically they had committed a serious crime while incarcerated at Alcatraz, such as an attempted escape or an assault on an officer. For example, Robert "Birdman" Stroud occupied D Block cell number forty-two on the third tier from 1942 to 1948. Due to his psychotic condition, officials moved Stroud to the prison hospital

Robert "Birdman" Stroud

While in federal prison at Leavenworth, Robert Stroud earned the name "Birdman" because of his dedication to birds. Stroud's criminal career began at age nineteen, when he murdered a bartender in Alaska. This earned him a twelve-year sentence at McNeil Island prison.

Stroud had an above-average IQ and could read and write in several languages, which he taught himself through correspondence classes.

At McNeil, he attacked and wounded another prisoner, which resulted in a transfer to Leavenworth prison

Leavenworth informally permitted inmates to keep small pets in their cells.

Stroud started with two sparrows that he found in the yard. Later he requested a canary. Eventually his bird collection grew to over two hundred. Using two adjoining cells, Stroud's birds were stacked in wine cages three rows high. He studied, bred, dissected, and sold the birds. His extensive research was compiled in a 483-page book, *Stroud's Digest on the Diseases of Birds*, which was published in 1943.

While at Leavenworth, Stroud stabbed and killed a guard, which resulted in a death sentence. His sentence was later reduced to life in prison in solitary confinement.

When Stroud transferred to Alcatraz in 1942, he could not have birds in his cell. Psychiatric evaluations proved him to be psychotic, and he sometimes suffered violent mood swings. He served six years in D Block isolation and another eleven years in the prison hospital.

In 1959 he transferred to the federal medical facility in Springfield, Missouri. He died there in 1963 at the age of seventy-three. In total, Stroud spent fifty-four years in prison with forty-four of the years served in solitary confinement.

Robert "Birdman" Stroud's cell today. Stroud spent fifty-four years of his life in prison.

where he stayed until 1959. In total, Stroud was in complete isolation for a total of forty-four years, counting time in other prisons.

After spending nineteen days in the hole, officers moved Quillen to an isolation cell on the segregated D Block. Quillen recounts this experience:

> Segregation was very boring and the days seemed endless. Even worse, there was far too much time to think. Because of the lack of activity, it was so easy to fall into a state of depression, brought about by our natural instinct to think back to better times of the past. It was also easy to think about how things could have been. . . .

> I managed to make the best of D Block for the first six weeks after release from the hole. I had partially adjusted to the routine of boredom and depression. I would walk, read and often sleep during the day to pass the time, but regardless of what I did, I could not relieve the terrible torment that seemed to rage within me. . . . I wanted somehow to relieve this rage by screaming, crying and destroying something. Despite my often expressed belief that "they couldn't break me," I felt I was slowing going insane.[47]

Quillen's stay in isolation was soon to be extended even longer. To vent his rage, Quillen and a number of other inmates staged a rebellion. The disturbance included raking their tin cups on the bars, breaking toilets and wash basins, then breaking barred cell windows by pitching porcelain chunks, ripping open mattresses and pillows and flinging the stuffing to the flats below, and finally, throwing lit rolls of toilet paper that started fires.

The all-night destruction resulted in swift and direct punishment from Warden Johnston.

Each inmate involved lost one-half of his good time and was sentenced to nineteen days in isolation—some in their destroyed cells, with a bucket for a toilet—followed by increased detention in D Block. The prisoners became ineligible for transfer to another institution until the damages were paid for and all forfeited good time had been restored.

Cell Block A

Today A Block still has the original flat bars from the military prison. Since it had not

A view of a cell in A Block, with the original soft-iron flat bars.

Transferred from Leavenworth prison in September 1934, Kelly was among the early groups of prisoners arriving at Alcatraz. He gained fame for the 1933 kidnapping of Charles Urschel, a millionaire oilman from Oklahoma. (Kelly used his mother's maiden name to avoid disgracing his family.)

The college-educated Kelly had a Catholic upbringing and had even served as an altar boy. He started his crime career in the liquor bootlegging business. Bank robberies followed.

Then, in search of a big "take," Kelly and his wife decided to kidnap a wealthy person. Four other people also participated in the nine-day sensational kidnapping: Albert Bates, Harvey Bailey, and Kelly's in-laws, who provided the farm where Urschel was held. After a two-hundred-thousand-dollar ransom was picked up, the kidnappers separated and traveled through sixteen different states. Kelly and his wife managed to stay free for fifty-six days before being arrested. Kelly, Bates, and Bailey were eventually sent to Alcatraz; his father-in-law was sent to Leavenworth; and his mother-in-law and wife went to another federal penitentiary.

A stable, sociable inmate while at Alcatraz, Kelly worked as a cobbler and later as a shop bookkeeper. In 1951 Kelly transferred to Leavenworth, where he died of a heart attack on his fifty-ninth birthday, July 17, 1954.

been remodeled, A Block was used only occasionally to isolate troublemakers. Inmates did push-ups, jumping jacks, and paces to keep warm in these cold, damp cells.

Being an inmate at Alcatraz for twenty-six years, Alvin Karpis experienced all of the levels of imprisonment, including the dungeon, the strip cell, and A Block solitary. Once he was involved in a yard fight and was beaten severely. But, because Karpis defiantly refused to tell a deputy warden the reason for the fight and also refused medical attention, he was sent to the A Block "hole." As Karpis writes,

It really isn't bad as far as holes go. I'm on the top tier of A Block with a solid door on the cell except that there is an eighteen-inch hole cut across the bottom of the door which is covered with heavy mesh wire screen. Every night I am handed two blankets which are picked up in the morning when I receive a piece of bread. I get three slices a day.[48]

In A Block, a prisoner could request an interview slip (or cop-out slip, as the convicts called it) enabling him to be released early if he promised to obey the rules. Karpis refused to make any promises, so his stay was longer than that of the other man involved in the fight.

In later years, A Block cells were used for storage of supplies rather than for prisoners.

Another Type of Segregation

During the early years, Alcatraz prison practiced race segregation. In 1935 there were only nine black inmates. They sat at their own table in the mess hall. The blacks even had a complete tier of cells to themselves, right above Fish Row. (*Fish* is the designated slang for new inmates.)

By 1949 the number of black convicts at Alcatraz had increased. As a result, in 1952, the prison tried integration. However, this effort brought much protest and rioting from white inmates. Integration was abandoned; by 1954 all black inmates were segregated on Broadway.

The Mess Hall

The most dangerous area in the cell house was the mess hall. Because inmates had eating utensils that could be used as weapons, officials were cautious to keep the area under control. So that the prisoners would not be tempted to overpower and disarm the

Guard Frank Heaney

At age twenty-one, Frank Heaney was the youngest man ever to serve as a correctional officer at Alcatraz. He served at Alcatraz from 1948 until 1951. After three years of correctional service, Heaney was ready for a

Frank Heaney was a guard at Alcatraz from 1948 to 1951.

career change. He was grateful to be recalled into active duty during the Korean War. After the war, Heaney embarked on a twenty-seven-year career as a fireman.

As a young boy growing up, Heaney sold newspapers with headlines that featured names of famous racketeers and their criminal activities. He enjoyed watching weekly gangster movies at the theater. Heaney was seven years old when Alcatraz opened its doors across the bay from Berkeley, where he lived. The prison enhanced his interest in notorious gangsters and eventually led him to seek employment at Alcatraz.

While at the Rock, Heaney found himself guarding some of the nation's toughest felons, including George "Machine Gun" Kelly, Alvin "Creepy" Karpis, and Robert "Birdman" Stroud. The job was not the Hollywood version Heaney had envisioned. A correctional officer's job was sometimes boring, sometimes demanding, and often terrifying. Because of Heaney's youthfulness, inmates tried to harass him psychologically with obscene remarks. Heaney shares his stories in a book, *Inside the Walls of Alcatraz*, and often autographs books for tourists in the Alcatraz bookshop. He has appeared on television and served as consultant for the fictional movies *Murder in the First* and *The Rock*.

floor guards, these officials did not carry guns or billy clubs. However, armed guards on exterior catwalks kept watch during mealtime. The punishment for fighting in the mess hall carried a flat five-hundred-day loss of good time.

Medical Facilities

Most inmates at one time or another experienced the "sick call" line and also used the hospital facilities within the cell house. Daily sick call followed the noon lunch break. Ill inmates lined up for a chance to see the medical technical assistant(MTA), who dispensed medications such as aspirins or cough medicine. If the illness required a doctor's diagnosis, the MTA added the inmate's name to a list for the chief medical officer to see on his daily two-hour visit to the cell house.

Guard Frank Heaney gave his impression of sick call:

Illnesses were exaggerated. . . . There was always a long line. I'd estimate ten percent of the prison population showed up daily. The first attendant they would see was the medical technician. He would give them a routine check, and maybe a doctor would prescribe sleeping pills, the drug they usually asked for. Many were in line *every day*. Maybe it was just to have something to do. Going up and bellyaching to a doc-

tor took some of the boredom away, or relieved the pressure of monotony.[49]

Dr. Richard Yocom, the commander of the Public Health Service, lived on the island. Yocom served all people on the island—prisoners as well as families. Warden Johnston insisted that the prison personnel and their families, who did not have immediate access to San Francisco's doctors and hospitals, should have continuous medical aid while on Alcatraz. The inmates liked and respected Yocom, and sick call was a pleasant diversion.

The hospital was located on the second level of the cell house above the mess hall. The MTA scheduled admittance to the hospital, and the inmate had to pass through several locked doorways and gates. The hospital included operating and X-ray rooms, treatment and sick rooms, as well as a psychiatric ward. A consulting dentist and other specialists visited the hospital regularly. If an inmate had a long-term illness, he would be transferred to the federal prison hospital in Springfield, Missouri.

In an effort to brighten the surroundings, Warden Johnston tried color psychology to relieve the dull drab reality of steel and concrete. The cell house was first painted with the combined colors of gray, green, and white; years later, startling pink and red replaced those colors. The mess hall was painted pink and ivory. Even the industrial shop areas were painted. Prisoners had no choice but to try to adapt themselves to their existence, colorful or not.

Routine, Routine, Routine

Life on the Rock was not easy. The most difficult part proved to be repeating the same routine over and over again. The Monday through Friday grind allowed only six minutes of daily conversation in the years when the rule of silence was enforced. From 1934 until 1937, inmates could speak on only three occasions: during mealtime to request salt, pepper, and sugar; in the yard on Saturdays; and for three minutes during a morning and afternoon work break (later extended to thirty minutes). The inmate's structured life required being in the proper place at the precise time every day.

Ruled by the Whistle

On weekdays, inmates stayed locked in their cells a minimum of fourteen hours. Working and eating used up the hours outside of the cells. When the island was blanketed in fog or the weather was too inclement, the routine was different. Inmates were not allowed to leave the cell house for their industry jobs on those days for fear of escape and they spent all day, except for meals, in their cells. Weekdays started with an ear-shattering bell at 6:30 A.M. ordering inmates to get out of bed, wash up at their cell basin, and tidy their cells. After standing for the body count, the prisoners walked single file to the mess hall block by block.

After a twenty-minute meal, a shrill whistle blast signaled inmates to stand. They turned in their fork and spoon as they exited and marched to the cell house, where they stood in front of their designated cells. Another whistle blast ordered the inmates to step inside their cage. All of the doors rolled shut behind them with a loud bang. With inmates facing their cell doors, guards counted them. A third whistle blast told them the count was over.

The next command opened the cell doors, and the inmates marched along their tier and down the circular stairs. They passed through a metal detector, or snitch box, which detected any metal pieces being taken from the cell house to the yard or work area. Painted lines on the yard pavement designated specific workshops. Once lined up, guards checked inmates' names against a roster sheet for each shop. If all was correct, the captain of the guard signaled the wall guard to lower the key that opened the yard wall gate. Each shop crew proceeded through the gate.

Inmate Jim Quillen shared his feelings about his first day at work:

> I can still recall the beauty that met my eyes as I stepped through the wall gate for the first time. The Golden Gate Bridge was directly in front of me and there were wisps of fog behind it. The bay was smooth and calm. To my left was San Francisco and to my right, Sausalito and Marin, all reminders of the normal life I had thrown away.[50]

The trek to the shops continued down two more flights of stairs, through another snitch box, and down a road. Once at the shop, the men changed into a different set of clothes suitable for their job. Guards locked all doors in the work area and took many head counts throughout the day.

Work stopped at 11:30 A.M., and inmates again changed clothes. Tired and hungry, the inmates plodded up the hill. Once there, the routine continued. Head count. Down to the mess hall. Eat lunch. March back to the cell. Another count. Back down the hill. Work stopped at 4:30

Inmates enter the mess hall for breakfast. During the prison's first few years, silence at mealtimes was strictly enforced and prisoners could only speak to request salt, pepper, or sugar.

P.M. Back up the hill. Head count. Supper. Back to the cell. At 5:30 P.M., cell doors clanged shut for thirteen hours.

Head Counts

Counting the men at Alcatraz was serious business, and guards conducted a count at least every thirty minutes. Inmate Karpis describes the many head counts throughout the day:

> We are counted in our cells in the morning. We are counted at breakfast. We are counted after breakfast. When we're back in our cells, we're recounted on the way out of the cell house onto the yard. We're counted going out the gate and down the cliff face to the industries. We're counted when we arrive at our work stations and,

when all the counts are called in and checked out, we are counted every half hour by the [officers] in charge of each industry who then phone in the count throughout the day.[51]

Filling a Four-Hour Gap Before Lights Out

Between 5:30 P.M. and 9:30 P.M., inmates could do whatever they wanted within the confines of their cell. They could write letters, read, study, and smoke. Later, when rules relaxed some, inmates were allowed to play musical instruments and paint oil pictures.

Because televisions, newspapers, and radios were not permitted, most inmates entertained themselves with books and magazines. Inmates did not go to the library, however.

An aerial view shows the prison industries and shops area, where many of the inmates worked. While on the job, inmates were counted by guards every half hour.

They had a catalog that listed over ten thousand books available in the library, and they requested books by filling out a form. Every day a library orderly delivered the ordered books to the prisoners' cells. In addition, inmates could order "approved" books (without sex, violence, or crime) and subscribe to magazines, the most popular being *Time*, *Life*, and *Newsweek*.

Karpis describes his first weekend night at Alcatraz:

> Not even 5:30 P.M. yet! What to do till "lights out"? I wish there was a commissary at Alcatraz as there is at all the other federal prisons. A candy bar or something sweet would help a lot.
>
> I browse through some late editions of *Time* and *Newsweek*, but there are missing pages and, in some cases, holes in the pages. Censorship! Any mention of crime has been removed.
>
> Looking out across the grey cell house from my vantage point on the third gallery, I see the cons in the cells across from me and below on the second tiers. They are either reading, writing a letter, or just sitting on the edge of their bunks smoking. Many of them stare hypnotically at one spot on the cell wall opposite them.
>
> Restlessly I try walking up and down in my cell but it makes me dizzy turning around so often. I sit down and try to read again but it's no use.[52]

Inmate Whitey Thompson grew to enjoy the sweet, mournful sounds of a harmonica as well as the strum of a guitar. In the 1950s the prison allowed inmates to play musical instruments such as the guitar, banjo, trumpet, and harmonica in their cells from 6:30 to 7:30 P.M.

Inmates could request books from Alcatraz's library, which contained over ten thousand titles.

Lights Out: The Long Night

Cell lights blinked off at 9:30 P.M. Guards counted the inmates throughout the night. They walked down the corridors and shone a flashlight in each cell to count each prisoner.

Prisoners at Alcatraz penitentiary eventually grew accustomed to many nighttime sounds. Some of them blended into their dreams, like the sound of two foghorns at opposite ends of the island that split the silence every twenty seconds and every thirty seconds. But one noise, so mentally upsetting to inmates, could not be blocked out.

Alcatraz strictly enforced its rules prohibiting pleasurable objects. Howard Needham discusses this in his book *Alcatraz*.

"'Inanimate' things from the outside world such as brand-name soap, candy, soft drinks, magazines and other canteen-type items were forbidden. Alcatraz had no PX [commissary] or canteen store. Money was forbidden in the hands of prisoners. There were no trustees. All items of a game nature and any object that could be construed as a potential device for gambling was contraband, and the sentence for possession meant time in one of the 'hole' cells and loss of good-time credits."

Almost nightly, the guards staged target practice outside the prison wall. The staccato noises of pistols, rifles, riot guns, and machine guns echoed in prisoners' ears. To prove their skilled marksmanship, guards intentionally left the bullet-pierced dummies lying around for the inmates to see the next day.

A Break in the Monotony

Mealtime offered a welcome break in the prisoners' monotonous day. The menu repeated itself about every ten days. Administrators claimed that the food at Alcatraz—thirty-six hundred calories per day—was the best in the federal prison system in its early years.

The dining, or mess, hall accommodated twelve tables on each side of the room and was divided by a center aisle. At mealtime, two single-file lines marched down the aisle to the steam table, where the lines split, one turning right, the other turning left. Inmates picked up a tray and a fork and spoon. Jim Quillen writes about the procedure:

As we passed along the steam table, we extended our trays to the inmate serving the line. He would give a measured portion of the food he was serving. If we did not want any particular dish, we were not obligated to take it, however, we were required to eat what we took or face disciplinary action.[53]

Random seating was not permitted in the dining hall. Inmates filed in according to the order of their cells and stood until ten men arrived—five on each side—before they sat down as one group. This table setup remained the same until around 1962, when tables that seated four replaced the long tables.

With the entire population in one room, the mess hall provided an ideal setting for inmate disturbances. Quillen tells of the risks:

The dining hall in any institution is a very volatile and dangerous area. Many murders and riots have occurred in this particular section of many prisons. Alcatraz was no exception to the rule, and both guards and inmates alike were always relieved when the whistle blew for the return of the men to their own individual cells. . . . I also believe that the very close proximity of the machine gun guard and a ceiling lined with ten tear gas cannisters (which could be released instantaneously) had a quieting effect on the population. [54]

Privileges

Cooperative inmates could avoid continuous lockup by choosing to work in various workshops or other areas of the prison, including the kitchen, hospital, library, gardens, or on the dock. Convicts treasured their jobs. Work was a privilege. Not only did a job break the monotony of prison life, it offered other incentives such as a small salary, accrument of "good time" (days deducted from their sentence), and an opportunity to socialize with other inmates.

Although the Rock did not have a formal reform program, Warden Johnston felt that work itself was a strong agent of reform. He said, "Just plain honest-to-goodness work [would] lessen mental strains . . . relax their tightly wound emotional threads."[55]

During the first thirty days of a prisoner's incarceration, only menial jobs were available to him, such as sweeping the cell house or cleaning up the exercise yard. Current inmates received job priority, and the new arrivals usually had to wait for an opening.

The main dining room in the prison. Meals provided a welcome break in the day but could also be dangerous, as violence sometimes erupted in the dining room.

In 1934 an act of Congress established the Federal Prison Industries. The purpose of prison industries was to manufacture products that would reduce the cost of retaining prisoners, create employment for inmates, and supply the military, other prisons, and government agencies with services at a lower-than-market cost. At Alcatraz, industries included a laundry and dry cleaning plant, mat factory, clothing factory, and a model shop.

Besides the penitentiary personnel, the laundry and dry cleaning plant served the U.S. transports and the U.S. Army posts in the San Francisco Bay area. Orders for the mat factory originated from the U.S. Navy Department for warships located on the Pacific Coast. The clothing factory trained inmates to make prison uniforms, civilian clothing for prisoners being released, and uniforms for custodial officers. In the model shop, inmates built furniture and reconditioned discarded government furniture.

About 50 percent of the Alcatraz inmate population worked in industries, which had 110 job positions. Prior to 1942 prisoners did not earn money. However, they did earn two to four days of credit time per month—which resulted in reduced sentences—in addition to the regulated good time already deducted from their sentence.

On the Job

Jim Quillen describes an assignment he took in the brush shop. The job, which he kept for six months, proved to be frustrating and boring:

An inmate welds a seam on a submarine net flotation buoy, one of several used to protect the bay from enemy submarines during World War II.

Enticements to Working in the Industries

In his book *Alcatraz from Inside*, inmate Jim Quillen explains the advantages of working in the prison industries. An inmate could earn both "good time" and money, which was placed in a savings account.

"An inducement for working in the industries was the opportunity to earn additional good time. Industrial good time was computed on the basis of two additional days each month for the first year, four days each month for the next three years and five days each month for the fifth and following years. For the inmate serving a short sentence, it was a great incentive. . . . [Around 1942] still another incentive was given the inmates to work in the industries: a pay scale. Jobs were graded into four groups. Men on grade one earned twelve cents per hour; grade two, ten cents; grade three, seven and one-half cents; and grade four paid five cents. It was not much, but it made the men feel they were being rewarded for their labor. . . . [However,] inmates were not afforded the privilege of a commissary [to] buy some of the minor luxuries such as a candy bar, . . . cookies and ready-made cigarettes. At Alcatraz the earned money could only be spent to buy a limited number of subscriptions to magazines, a musical instrument, dominoes or bridge [books]. . . . The pay scale was later upgraded to seventeen and one-half [cents] for maximum and six cents for minimum."

To make a hair brush, the type used to sweep long corridors, an inmate was supplied with a board with a hundred or more tapered holes drilled in it, a crochet hook, a spool of very fine copper wire, a vise and two pounds of horse hair. You clamped the board in a vise, pushed the hook through the hole, pulled the wire through the hole so it was double, opened the loop in the wire, then pulled the wire taut until the hair doubled over and seated itself in the tapered hole, without breaking the fine copper wire. This procedure was repeated over and over again, until all the holes were filled and the wire was tied off so all the hair could not fall out of the brush. A cap was screwed over the face of the wire, the brush was trimmed so that all the hair was even and the brush was complete! Picture doing that over and over again for seven hours a day, five days a week![56]

In *Escape from Alcatraz*, author J. Campbell Bruce describes work done at Alcatraz during World War II:

The war spirit reached into the prison, and the convicts, imbued with patriotism, rallied to do their part. The laundry did mountains of wash for the military: San Francisco was a teeming port of embarkation for the South Pacific Theater. The tailor shop turned out tens of thousands of trousers for the Army. Convict machinists and welders did repair work for the Navy, particularly on the buoys for the antisubmarine nets in the bay.[57]

Prime Jobs

Although industry jobs paid inmates with time credit, other jobs within the prison granted different privileges. For example, a work assignment as a deliveryman for the prison library allowed greater freedom of movement within the cell house. Inmates relished any freedom. The library orderly delivered books and magazines to cells (up to seven items per cell) on a wheeled table. In making deliveries, he often enjoyed brief conversations with other inmates without being subject to punishment.

Inmates deemed kitchen, or culinary, detail a "soft touch." The kitchen job allowed prisoners additional perks, including use of the yard every afternoon and as much food as they wanted. The seven-day culinary workday ran from 6:00 A.M. to 6:00 P.M. with breaks after completing assigned tasks. In 1940 Alvin Karpis compared his new job in the kitchen to his former job in the laundry:

> I am put to work on the steam table in the dining room. Myself and five others have to pick up the silverware and trays, clean the tables after each meal and mop the floor. There is nothing to the job.
>
> The kitchen is like a luxury hotel compared to the mangle in the laundry. The first morning I have two eggs and strawberry preserves for breakfast. My friends Sawyer, Weaver, and Boxhead Brown are working in the butcher shop thus I can have my choice of meat cuts anytime of the day. Filet Mignon becomes a part of my regular diet.[58]

Jobs vs. Control

Sometimes inmates used the power of their jobs to induce a change in prison rules. For example, inmates went on strike (conducted a work stoppage) against the no-talking reg-

Inmates Revolt to Change the Silence Rule

On January 22, 1936, about half of the population of 250 inmates went on a work strike to protest the silence rule. As punishment, the prison administration fed the convicts only bread and water. After three days, the prisoners returned to work with the rule unchanged.

In 1937, a second work strike took place, this time involving all of the inmates. At a signaled time, all prisoners dropped their tools and shouted "We want to talk! We want newspapers! We want radios!" But Warden Johnston's edict was no work, no food. The inmates were locked up and placed on bread and water. The cell house echoed with shouts, banging tin cups, slammed table tops, and clanging chained beds. By the end of a week, most of the convicts tired of the skimpy diet and returned to their jobs. The leaders of this strike were thrown in the dungeon.

Later that year several inmates in the dining room broke into conversation at separate tables, and the forbidden activity began to spread throughout the room. Not knowing who to apprehend because so many were breaking the rule, the guards were helpless. In addition, the eight dungeon cells could not house everybody. Thus, the rule of silence on the Rock ceased. Warden Johnston announced to the press that he abolished the rule to ease the rigidity of discipline. The press praised Johnston for the humanitarian gesture.

Kitchen employees pass through the food line. Working in the kitchen was one of the most coveted jobs in the prison.

ulation. During the prison's first three years, inmates revolted two times in an effort to get the silence command revoked. Each time, the participants endured bread-and-water diets for three to five days. And, each time, the regulation remained in force. However, inmates still rebelled against the rule. Finally, in 1937, inmates unwilling to endure the silence any longer began talking spontaneously in the dining hall. The incessant chatter finally convinced the warden to drop the rigid rule.

Most prisoners tried to find ways to make life more endurable while serving time. However, some prisoners could not make the adjustment. J. Campbell Bruce relates how one inmate expressed his despair:

Rufe Persful, Arkansas robber was working with the dock gang. He laid his left hand on a block and chopped off the fingers with a hatchet, one after the other, like a butcher cleaving chops off a pork loin. He then offered the hatchet to a gaping convict, laid his right hand on the block and said, "Chop them off, too!" The convict flung the hatchet aside and ran shouting to the guard.[59]

However, the majority of inmates found ways to avoid such extreme depression. For example, those who cooperated found that other privileges besides work could enrich their stay. Sometimes, such simple things as showers and shaves raised their spirits. Receiving mail and conversing with visitors helped, too.

Inmates' Leisure Time: Life by the Book

Freedom from work did not mean freedom from a timetable. Time in the recreation yard and even time for bathing and shaving was strictly regimented. If desired, inmates could partake in bimonthly movies, weekly religious services, and have monthly visitors. To maintain their sanity and relieve boredom, some inmates took college correspondence courses. Others learned to play musical instruments and to oil paint. Whether daily, weekly, or monthly, all activities had a designated time and place.

Bathing and Shaving

Twice a week, inmates marched to the shower room. Following a shower, each inmate walked through a long shallow tank filled with a disinfectant solution to prevent the spread of athlete's foot. A guard checked off the name and number of the inmate.

Donning bathrobes and backless slippers, inmates picked up a clean set of clothes. The next counter held household supplies such as toilet paper, matches, envelopes, writing pa-

Inmates showered twice a week in this shower room while guards kept watch.

The prisoners looked forward to the few hours each week they were allowed to spend in the recreation yard, where they could play baseball, cards, or just sit and socialize.

per, bar soap, and tooth powder. Having made their selections, inmates marched back to their cells to dress and wait for a count.

Officer Frank Heaney relates the procedure for shaving, which was required three times a week:

> Shaving was strictly enforced. When I worked the 4:00 P.M. to midnight shift, one of my responsibilities was to issue a razor blade to each inmate. He could keep it inside his cell for thirty minutes only. I had a small board with a hook on the end and, sometime around 6:30 P.M., I'd go to each inmate and put his blade on the lip of the cell. Exactly one half-hour later, they'd better have that blade back in place. Otherwise, it was solitary confinement.

We supplied all inmates with cheap little double-edged razor blades and a sharpening device, a small piece of leather.

They each had a shaving mug, but some just preferred to use soap and water.

> If an inmate refused to shave—and on occasion one would—three or four officers would be called in to hold him down for a dry shave, as an example for the other inmates. If you've ever had a dry shave with a cheap government-issue blade, you know why we didn't have that problem too often.[60]

After the weekday monotony of dull activities, the weekend brought a welcome change in routine. Weekends were set aside for time in the recreation yard for most inmates.

The Recreation Yard

The recreation yard was a cement site enclosed by twenty-foot walls and contained a set of concrete bleachers. Armed officers, using a wraparound catwalk and squat gun boxes, policed the yard. Chilling temperatures and harsh winds prevailed in the recreation yard.

The kitchen crew and those in isolation used the yard Monday through Friday. All others, unless they were being disciplined, used it on Saturday and Sunday for two and a half hours each day. Morton Sobell, a former inmate on Alcatraz, describes the liberation of the recreation yard:

> You could do what you wanted to do. You could sit on the steps and talk or watch. You could walk. You could play cards. You had a choice here [in the recreation yard] which you didn't have back there [in the cell house]. . . . [The recreation yard] was freedom, freedom to do what you wanted to do.[61]

The recreation area was slightly smaller than a football field, and inmates playing different sports often collided with each other. When playing softball or handball, the games lasted only as long as the balls stayed inside the yard. Prisoner Karpis related his first experience in the yard on August 15, 1936:

> I'm anxious and excited as work ends for the week. Now I can get on the yard. Saturday afternoons and Sunday mornings are yard days which means the entire general population is loose in the cement arena. "The Yard" at Alcatraz is more than an exercise area, it is an experience—often a dangerous experience, sometimes a fatal experience—always an unpredictable one.
>
> At this time of the year the yard is always cold and the wind increases steadily in velocity as the afternoon grows late. The sand and dirt swirls around the clustered figures in the cold courtyard as we sit on

the steps trying to roll and light our smokes. There's always a ball game in progress and the danger of being hit by a fastball or dumped on your ass by an anxious outfielder trying to snare it keeps everyone alert. At the other end of the yard are two handball courts and two horseshoe pits getting plenty of action.[62]

Additional Yard Activities

Other games allowed in the yard included bridge, checkers, dominoes, and chess. The most popular game was bridge. However, instead of cards, the prisoners used specially marked dominoes. (Regular playing cards were banned in prisons because of their celluloid content, which the convicts could grind up and use as an explosive.)

The dominoes were held by special boards that allowed a player to see his own "cards" but not his opponents'. Almost all inmates played bridge at some level. But to several inmates, the game became an escape to another world. The men played with enthusiasm, vigor, and humor, temporarily forgetting the reality of their lives within those cement walls. Quillen, who often played bridge, recalls,

> *Culbertson's Beginners' Book of Bridge* was beyond a doubt the most desired and read book in the prison's twenty-nine years of existence. When the Warden permitted "Auto Bridge" (a device where an inmate could play the game by himself) to be ordered, it was to some inmates like Christmas had happened twice in one year.[63]

Some prisoners used this yard freedom to plan escapes, riots, and fights. Animosity between prisoners ran high, and usually grievances

The Hierarchy in the Exercise Yard

In *Riddle of the Rock*, author Don DeNevi describes the ranking of the prisoners in the exercise yard. Long-term prisoners Joe Carnes and Bumpy Johnson are cited as examples.

"In the exercise yard Carnes waited for Bumpy Johnson to come out. . . . The two men played chess every Saturday on the top row of the 'bleachers,' the concrete terraces in the Alcatraz recreation yard that looked like giant steps leading up from the yard to the blank wall of the prison building. The steps were part of a huge retaining wall and foundation supporting the cellhouse. Inmates used the steps as seats from which they could view the handball courts and softball diamond and, in general, scan the entire recreation yard. The top step was reserved for only the most revered or feared cons, or maybe both. Having earned the privilege of sitting there meant you were always in the sun, if there was any sunshine to be had, compared with sitting on the lower, cold steps, where the sunlight was blocked by the high walls of the yard. From the top step an inmate could see over the walls. There was a panoramic view of San Francisco Bay, the San Francisco city skyline, the Golden Gate Bridge, and Sausalito.

The top step belonged to Bumpy Johnson. Any con who dared join Bumpy and Joe Carnes up there without Bumpy's approval was foolish. Sooner or later he would receive a severe beating or a knife puncture."

These large concrete steps were used as bleachers from which the inmates could view the entire yard. The top step was reserved for the most respected and feared inmates.

were dealt with in the exercise yard. When an inmate wanted to settle a grudge, he summoned his buddies to surround that person while he stabbed his victim with a form of knife—a sharpened fork, spoon, or wooden instrument. Then the group withdrew from the scene—leaving the bleeding victim lying there.

In such an incident, the inmates rarely received punishment since no amount of questioning resulted in answers about who did it or why. The number one rule among inmates was that "you never tell." Author Don DeNevi explaines the code of behavior for older, experienced convicts: "Men had died rather than rat on another con. They had been tortured, hanged, beaten to death, and electrocuted—and still not ratted."[64]

The Chapel at Alcatraz

Although the yard provided physical release from pent-up energy, some inmates needed spiritual nourishing, too. Religious services held by visiting chaplains offered spiritual solace to the men. Occasionally a Protestant chaplain lived on the island. Jewish services were offered on Saturdays; Catholic and

This building was the chapel when Alcatraz was a military prison. Later it served as living quarters for bachelor correctional officers.

Al Capone's Mother Visits

Al Capone was among the first trainload of inmates who arrived at the penitentiary. In his book *Inside the Walls of Alcatraz*, guard Frank Heaney relates a visitor's frustration at the security system.

"Of course, all visitors who even landed at the dock had to go through a metal detector. One of the first stories I heard at Alcatraz was about Al Capone's mother and the metal detector. When she came to visit her son for the first time, she of course had to pass through the security system, and when she got to the metal detector, it went off. She went through again and it still kept buzzing. Finally, she was told the only way she would be allowed to enter was to have a security search, and so she was escorted to a dressing room by an officer's wife.

They found that the metal stays[supports] in her corset were setting off the alarm. It embarrassed her no end. When she reached the visiting area, she was plenty excited, and met her son with a volley of her native language, Italian. Of course, that wasn't allowed either. She was so upset by the embarrassment of the security check and her language problem, that she never returned to see her son on Alcatraz."

Protestant inmates worshiped on Sundays. The warden did not allow officers, who guarded prisoners during the chapel services, to participate.

If an inmate attended church services, he forfeited equal time from his recreation in the yard. Otherwise, the warden believed that inmates would attend chapel just to get out of their cells for an hour. Years later, at the insistence of a priest, the penalty for church attendance was removed. To the surprise of the warden, the attendance at religious services remained at 10 percent of the population.

The chapel served as a dual-purpose room where inmates also viewed monthly movies (twice monthly after 1950) shown on a dropped screen in front of the altar. Only prisoners in good standing saw the movies—mostly western and musical comedy films. D Block inmates were excluded from this privilege.

Beyond movies, religious services, and the exercise yard, a prisoner could look forward to visitors and correspondence with family and friends.

Visitors

When Alcatraz first opened, only one visitor per month was allowed. Only blood relatives, wives, and lawyers could visit—no friends, girlfriends, or fiancées. Visitors could not shake hands with prisoners or touch them in any way. They communicated on a telephone separated by a thick glass partition. During the forty-five-minute visit, only family concerns could be discussed—never such things as current events. Prison officers, who stood behind both the prisoner and the visitor, monitored the conversations and cut the phone connection if these rules were broken.

All visitors to Alcatraz had to submit a request in writing to the warden. Donald J. Hurley, whose father was a correctional officer at Alcatraz, describes the procedure after applying for a visit:

When approved, the warden would send a letter back to the party advising them to be on the dock at Pier 4 in San Francisco with the letter to show the boat officer. Once on

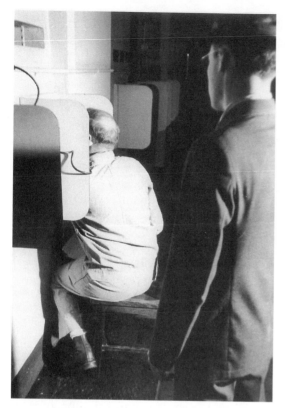

An inmate talks to a visitor on a phone while a guard monitors their conversation.

spondence. His parents learned about his imprisonment at Alcatraz from a priest. Quillen describes this emotional first visit from his parents, which had such a positive affect on him:

> When I reached the booth, I immediately peered through the glass. There sat my father and stepmother, crying as though their hearts would break. . . . All the bitterness and antagonism of the past years was washed away with that flood of tears, to be replaced by love, kindness and encouragement. I was so nervous and overjoyed, yet trembling so violently. . . . My first words must have been indistinguishable, as my mouth was so dry and the tears so profuse, I could hardly speak. It took several minutes before we were able to assume a rational conversation and this was periodically interrupted by unexpected spells of crying on both sides.

the island, the visitor would be transported by vehicle up to the prison. He or she would then walk through a full-body metal detector. The visit was conducted through one of five visitor stations by talking into phones and looking at each other through five inches of bullet-proof glass.[65]

Later, visitor restrictions relaxed. Visiting time increased to two hours per month and included relatives and close friends.

Complex Feelings

Jim Quillen had been at Alcatraz for several years without receiving any visitors or corre-

> Gone was the tough, independent and self-sufficient convict and in his place was a joyful, emotional man who was determined never to inflict pain, hurt or suffering on his family again. . . . In that moment, when I saw their tears and anguish, a new man was born. A man who was determined to forget the ways of the past and use every fiber of his body to make amends for his past mistakes. . . . I would make a whole-hearted effort to do something that would give them hope and peace about the future.

> In that short span of time, any thoughts of escape or suicide vanished. Nothing I would do in the future would hurt them.[66]

Mail

Each prisoner could receive three letters per week. Author Marilyn Tower Oliver tells how mail was stringently handled:

> Prisoners' mail was censored, and prisoners could only receive packages containing personal items. To keep them from receiving letters with coded or invisible messages, prisoners did not receive the original letters, but copies typed by Alcatraz staff. This also kept the prisoners from receiving mail that might contain paper that had been soaked with narcotics.[67]

Many times a prisoner received a typewritten letter with dotted lines where words had been deleted. The prisoner could only guess at what information was missing.

Allowed to write just one two-page letter each week, prisoners could correspond with only a blood relative. However, even inmates' letters were censored and rewritten by the staff of Alcatraz, leaving out any material that was considered a threat to the institution.

Added Privileges

Each year Alcatraz penitentiary added privileges. Beginning in 1935, twelve correspondence courses from the University of California Extension Program were made available to prisoners. Eighty-one inmates enrolled the first year. The next year, Alcatraz inmates could choose from twenty courses including English, French, Spanish, arithmetic, algebra, music, literature, and vegetable gardening.

Beginning in 1938, "good time" increased from two days a month to four days, inmates could order twenty magazines a year instead of twenty-dollars' worth, and they could request as many fiction books as they wanted during a week. After 1942, when prisoners began to earn money in industries, they could purchase a musical instrument or art supplies. The easing-up of rules began with Warden

Coping with Prison

Men in penitentiaries develop a variety of attitudes, including realistic, indifferent, vengeful, guilt-ridden, and insane ones. In the book *I Chose Prison*, author James V. Bennett quotes prisoner Stanley E. Mockford, who talks about how inmates cope with being locked up.

"The prisoner who has evolved a personal method of overcoming the more obvious difficulties of prison life, utilizes many devices to occupy his mind. Light reading is the commonest resource, or writing, about anything. Or conversation. Painting becomes an obsession for some men and so absorbed do they become in their hobby that time sometimes races too madly. Bridge seems to intrigue many. Building castles in the air. Daydreams. Sports—including the endless compiling of sports statistics and facts. Sleep is the great narcotic. In slumber, a prisoner is free—a circumstance that leads some prisoners to develop a great capacity for oblivion. They drift away into unconsciousness shortly after they reach their cells and live on a schedule divided between work and sleep."

Johnston and continued with each succeeding warden.

In 1946 George Harris, a San Francisco muralist, taught a Saturday class at the prison. Three years later, Harris entered thirty-four inmate works—oils, watercolors, and drawings—in San Francisco's annual Open Air Art Show in Union Square. This experience elevated the self-esteem of participating artists.

Inmates also taught each other how to play musical instruments. Some of the instruments included guitars, trumpets, and saxophones. Several inmates formed a band, which played for holidays and special occasions.

In 1950 Associate Warden Paul J. Madigan set aside a small recording facility in the basement of Alcatraz. The equipment allowed the inmates to record a message or a song and send it to wives, children, parents, or friends. The fifty-cent discs became popular, allowing inmates who did not write letters to maintain personal contact with loved ones.

In 1955 inmates welcomed another new idea. Bureau of Prisons director James V.

Bennett suggested the installation of radio outlets in the cells. Inmates were given earphones to enjoy two light music stations and, later, baseball broadcasts. The baseball games led to wagering, but not for money; instead, inmates wagered a hundred pushups or a hundred tailor-made cigarettes. Although the inmates never heard newscasts, they were gratified with the radio addition.

Holidays

Holidays were not cheerful times in prison. But the staff did recognize Christmas with token gifts to the prisoners. Prisoner Karpis describes Christmas Eve in 1941:

> Today Christmas packages are given to the cons at Alcatraz for the first time. They contain candy, cookies, and packaged cigarettes which are not available in Alcatraz through the year. All the contents must be used by the end of January or they will be considered contraband.[68]

Relaxed Rules and Hobbies

There were no official announcements, but there must have been meetings between Warden Johnston and the directors of the Bureau of Prisons. Prison reform was on the agenda. In *Alcatraz*, author Howard Needham summarized the changes during Alcatraz's first fourteen years under Warden Johnston.

"By 1937 the 'Rule of Silence' had been eliminated. In 1945 the men could see one movie a month in an improvised prison theater. A library had been organized, with fiction, reference and periodical sections . . . and there was a prison band.

As early as 1940 the mail restrictions were relaxed. Inmates could correspond with two relatives instead of just one. When Warden Johnston retired in 1948 inmates in good standing could pursue approved projects and hobbies in their cells. More, they could keep the equipment for those pursuits in their cubicles, including their own books, drawing materials, writing paper and learning aids. They could relieve the barren walls of their five-by-eight 'rooms' with pictures, religious objects and other approved decorations."

Prisoners playing saxophones and trumpets are led by a fellow inmate on a trombone. The inmate band played for holidays and special occasions.

In 1948 the first Christmas tree ever allowed in the prison was set up in the dining hall. The soft pine scent aroused long-forgotten emotions in inmates. In 1957 Warden Madigan added six cigars to the Christmas loot, and two years later, inmates could buy a blissful treat of a two-pound box of chocolates if they had two dollars in their account. Special Thanksgiving and Christmas meals were also added.

Even with all of the added privileges, some inmates still could not change their attitudes or follow the rigid regulations. They chose to break prison rules and, in some cases, schemed to escape; they were then forced to suffer the consequences.

Breaking Prison Rules

Inmates did not have far to look for reasons to rebel. Rules, in general, annoyed them. In order to get a rule changed, prisoners had to initiate a strike or a prison riot before the warden and his staff would respond. For example, by refusing to work, inmates showed their discontent with the silence rule, and after two strikes in three years, the administration revoked the rule.

Group Action

In time, inmates came to believe that they received more immediate consideration from the administration when they acted as a group. Guard Frank Heaney describes a dining room demonstration that he witnessed:

> All of a sudden the inmates started picking up the benches and tables, and their silverware and trays, and throwing them all over the place. Before long it was a full-scale riot. . . . It was obviously premeditated.
>
> The lieutenant on duty took one look at me and another officer, and told us to pick up a couple of rifles and go man the gun gallery outside the dining room. Believe me, I was glad to be on the outside.
>
> When the disturbance continued, we were ordered to break the glass and shove our rifles through to intimidate the prisoners. . . .

This particular episode lasted for over a half hour, which is quite a long time for a demonstration. We were ready at all times to trigger the teargas canisters mounted on the walls. If that had happened, the next step would have been to try to get gas masks in to the officers trapped inside. Fortunately, that didn't come about and we were able to quiet the inmates down.[69]

The riot failed to resolve anything, however, and officials punished all inmates with a one-week lockdown. This meant no work, no activities, no leaving the cell. For meals, officers delivered sandwiches to cells. Ringleaders of the melee served time in solitary and isolation.

Defiance Sometimes Works

Inmates also protested by refusing to eat. Prison hunger strikes sometimes imply dissatisfaction with the food, but at Alcatraz, that was not the case. Anytime inmates declined to leave their cells for the dining room, the staff suspected that a revolt to change something was in the planning stages.

A strange event took place in 1940. There was no riot, no noise, and no strike. But, for one week, the inmates invoked voluntary silence and also refused cooked food. They wordlessly did their jobs; filed silently to the mess hall; passed by the steam table, taking only a slice of bread and coffee; and ate silently. When word leaked to the public of this behavior, Warden Johnston gave a terse reply to the press, "It's the reaction of frustrated men. You lock a man up in a hotel for sixty, seventy, even ninety-nine years, and every so often he will seek to gain the attention of the world outside."[70]

In fact, this particular time, convicts at Alcatraz wanted access to San Francisco courts. They charged that their various petitions were not getting off the island. The reason for the prisoners' behavior may have been mysterious to outsiders, but prison officials, despite their public denials, understood it very well.

During Warden Edwin Swope's tenure (1948–1955), a rebellion by inmates forced a change from the coverall prison uniform to blue denim trousers and chambray shirts. Author J. Campbell Bruce explains:

Inmate riots resulted in lockdown, where they were confined to their cells and the privileges of work and activities were revoked.

Macaroni Broil

In 1951, due to budget limits, prison meals became repetitious, unattractive, and non-nutritious. Milk was watered down, and bologna was on the menu all too often. The dull menu repeated itself about every ten days. When a fat-laden "meat sauce" dish (composed of two pounds beef and twenty-eight pounds of beef fat) called "macaroni milanaise" arrived, a planned dining hall melee exploded. In his book *On the Rock*, inmate Alvin Karpis describes the frolic.

"Two cons run up each side of the center isle tipping over every table in the dining hall. The 'macaroni milanaise á la grease' flies in all directions, splattering cons and guards alike. Trays, silverware, plates and bread pudding are flung across the room as the multitude of bodies struggles to keep its footing on the greasy floor. The more intel-ligent cons in the room sit down and refuse to slip or slide in the rolling mess of food decorating the mess hall. Everyone in the room is sprinkled with macaroni from hair to shoes."

While attempting to restore order, the officers began slipping and sliding across the greasy floor—much to the delight of the cheering raucous inmates. But the officers finally convinced the convicts to return to their cells. Within days, the chief kitchen steward resigned under the pressure of trying to serve decent, tasty meals with an inadequate budget. One of the incident's ringleaders, feeling depressed because the fiasco was not supported by his fellow inmates, committed suicide with razor cuts around the armpits and groin arteries while confined in isolation.

One evening a convict flung his coveralls out onto Broadway and shouted to the officer on the floor, "You can shove 'em!" Soon the hated garments were flying from all the tiers. Artists shook out bottles of turpentine, then a convict threw a flaming roll of toilet paper from a top-tier cell. Broadway blazed merrily, bright as its namesake. And the men were measured for trousers.[71]

Festering Problems

Around 1949 the convicts transferred to Alcatraz included more blacks than whites. All new arrivals, whatever their race, needed to prove to the other inmates that they were tough. This resulted in weeks and months of fistfights. At this time the fights were confined to whites against whites and blacks against blacks. It was common to see food trays dropped on heads or pitchers of hot coffee splashed into faces.

Later, problems began to surface between the two races. Alvin Karpis reveals his thoughts on intermingling blacks and whites at Alcatraz:

My own feelings are mixed. I know [Warden] Swope is only using the integration as a further test of how far he can force us into submission. On the other hand, I recognize that the negroes who have arrived on Fish Row have probably got more class than the white trash beside them. I started my prison experiences years ago in a state system where integration was in full force so the concept is neither shocking nor upsetting to me.

Still, my instincts warn me that the mixture of white and black in the explosive atmosphere of Alcatraz will bring disaster.[72]

Whites vs. Blacks

In 1952 the growing number of blacks at Alcatraz upset some white inmates. A few whites—about twenty—objected to living in a cell next to or even opposite a black inmate. Because authorities in those years did not allow the prisoners to choose their own cells,

trouble was inevitable. Finally, after the supper lockup one night, the pent-up resentment erupted. Violent bedlam shook Alcatraz cellhouse walls: cursing; banging on bars; bed slamming; breaking toilets and sinks; and pitching flaming sheets and clothes into corridors. Karpis describes the incident further:

> The screws [officers] are unable to put out the fires for fear of being hit by flying debris. Within ten minutes the smoke is suffocating the cons on the flat and rolling in grey clouds up to the tiers. . . . Cries come up from the lower cells

A black man suspected of murder is placed under arrest. The increasing number of black inmates in the 1950s added racial tension to the already explosive atmosphere on Alcatraz.

A New Guard's Experience

In *Inside the Walls of Alcatraz*, Officer Frank Heaney described his first day at work and how the inmates tried to bully him.

"I had my first lesson in dealing with intimidation [threats] my first day on duty. I was walking down Broadway, the main corridor between the triple-tiered cell blocks in the main cell house, and suddenly every inmate along the walkway started whistling and making obscene remarks.

I asked one of the older guards how to deal with it. He said there was only one way: Ignore them. If you respond at all, they'll know they got to you and they'll never let up.

I wasn't really frightened, but I was so young and so new that at first the prison atmosphere did intimidate me. And I was bothered by the inmates' passive harassment. I had been told inmates wouldn't attack you unless you stood between them and freedom, or if you agitated them excessively. But though the prisoners knew just how far they could go, I didn't."

hidden below clouds of smoke. "We're all going to suffocate down here if we don't get rid of this smoke!"

"Plug up your toilets! Keep your foot on the flusher and let them overflow! That will flood out the fire!" shouts a con.

Everyone overflows his toilet and the salt water from San Francisco Bay comes flooding into the cell house. . . .

Fast-moving rapids of seawater plunge down the staircases at either end as the entire cell house fills with a cooling swirling tide which gradually extinguishes the flames. . . . It plunges in Niagara-like arcs from the second and third tiers into the deepening lake now covering the main cell-house floor. . . . The rioting continues another night although there is little left to throw out on the galleries.[73]

After two days of rampage, the whites won their case. The Broadway corridor now housed black convicts in the inside cells of B Block. C Block facing Broadway was reserved for quarantine of new prisoners. Blacks also endured segregation in the dining room, barbershop, showers, and the movies.

By 1954 half of the population was black, creating a shortage of cells for blacks. Warden Swope sometimes forced a few white men to occupy cells on Broadway beside or across from blacks as punishment. But to keep another racial riot from breaking out, the warden kept blacks out of the outside cells of B and C Blocks, which were now the exclusive white suburbs of Alcatraz.

Pleas for a Commissary

Around 1958 inmates decided that they wanted a commissary, similar to other prisons, where they could buy candy, cigarettes, and toiletries. The men craved sweets, and they wanted decent shampoo and soap. However, the administration adamantly opposed this privilege.

Consequently, the inmates went on a work strike that lasted eighteen days. No one left his cell. To discourage this strike, the staff served meals of peanut butter sandwiches on dry bread. But the inmates refused to eat the sandwiches and tossed them out of their cells. The corridors were piled with thousands of stale sandwiches before the strike ended.

During the strike, some inmates labeled as ringleaders were taken to the treatment unit, or D Block. There, seventeen prisoners sliced their Achilles' heel tendons with smuggled-in razor blades. This act allowed them to leave D Block and enter the prison hospital. They made painful hops on one foot, or if both heels were sliced, the men had to drag themselves to the hospital, which was above the mess hall. The inmates' tissues were su-

tured, their legs put in casts, and the men returned to the treatment unit.

On the eighteenth day, word was passed from cell to cell that all "good time" would be forfeited if the strike did not end. In support of the old-timers, who had earned many years of good time, the inmates went back to work. The strike was all in vain because Alcatraz never did get a commissary.

Snitch Boxes

Besides using food as a method of control, officers had other ways of maintaining order.

Supplies are unloaded at Alcatraz. Incoming supplies were passed through metal detectors to screen for breakout tools.

One security tactic that wore on the nerves of prisoners was the constant check for breakout tools. Inmates were forced to pass through metal detectors at least six times each day on their way to various activities. The electronic stool pigeons, also known as snitch boxes, were presumed to be infallible in detecting small pieces of metal.

Often, however, men passed through with knives or tools undetected in their pockets. To prevent this, the officers kept the machine set at a very high sensitivity level. Once, it was so high that the alarm sounded for every man coming out of the laundry. Suspecting a mutiny, the guards jerked each man out of line and searched him. It took hours to locate the trouble: metal eyelets in the convicts' shoes.

Because the guards did not entirely trust the machine, they stopped every twelfth man and searched him whether the alarm sounded or not. Likewise, if a guard wanted to punish, embarrass, or humiliate a prisoner whom he personally disliked, he could intentionally trip the alarm as the prisoner passed through. Prisoners resented this harassment in front of their peers and hated and feared the snitch box. Jim Quillen describes what happened at snitch boxes:

> If the alarm was triggered, the inmate was pulled out of line and given a shakedown (patted over his entire body to determine if he was carrying contraband). He was then again sent through the snitch box, and if he was unfortunate enough to trigger the alarm again, he was subjected to a "skin search." This entailed stripping to the bare skin, while the guards searched every seam and inch of clothing. The inmate was personally examined from top to bottom, including the soles of his feet, while his peers observed as they passed by. Not only

was this a disturbing incident mentally, in the winter, it was also physically painful. The cold, wet wind, which blew from the ocean, would leave one so cold that it often took hours to feel warm again.[74]

In 1958, the first time that inmate Whitey Thompson walked through the portable snitch box, the buzzer sounded. An officer took him aside and, after a shakedown, pulled a pack of cigarettes from Thompson's shirt pocket and told him to pass through the box again. This time, the buzzer was silent. The officer told Thompson to slide his cigarette package to the side of the electronic box and retrieve it after he passed through. The aluminum foil on the package had caused the problem.

Cell Shakedowns

In the eyes of inmates, guards were zany about security. Guards primarily worried about knives, which could be made out of such things as tableware, nail files, pieces of steel, scissors halves, pen parts, and screwdrivers. Guards implemented cell shakedowns when the prisoners were either at work or out in the yard. One guard, George Gregory, later told how he performed a cell shakedown in search of contraband:

> I would take the books, rifle through them, 'cause they can often cut the pages out of the inside and hide things in there. And then I'd go through their clothing, me-tic-u-lous-ly. Then their bed, of course. And also some beds had hollow legs and you had to check on that because they could put stuff up [there]. And shake every blanket down, and to the best you can, you'd check the mattress, especially

check for rips or a new sewing job. And also, we'd periodically take the mattress out and run 'em through a metal detector, and change mattresses.[75]

Inmates knew that they were victims of a shakedown when they returned to their cells and found all of their possessions jumbled in a heap on the floor.

Guards also performed periodic checks on cell bars. They used rubber mallets to tap on every bar of each man's cell. If a bar sounded different, guards inspected it thoroughly for filings.

Progressive Punishment

Punishment in prison was progressive. At Alcatraz, for example, a prisoner received a warning for his first minor infraction. For a second infraction, the prisoner might lose yard privileges or his job. Solitary confinement came next. But the worst punishment was to lose "good time."

By the 1940s, "good time" had increased to ten days off a sentence for every forty days of good behavior. And if an inmate also worked in industries, it was possible for him to earn up to five additional days off per month.

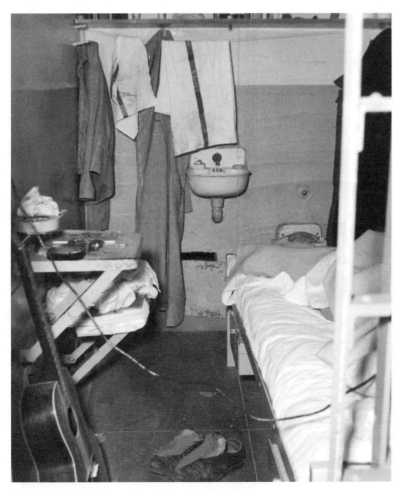

During shakedowns, guards looked through any possible hiding place for contraband. Here, a cell is left in disarray after a shakedown.

Breaking Prison Rules **73**

Deserted by his mother at age seven, Jim Quillen's childhood followed a pattern of living in boarding houses and running away. In his teen years he became involved in robberies and burglaries, ending up in a reformatory. More armed robberies landed Quillen in California's San Quentin prison, at age twenty-one. He spent the next eighteen years in three prisons, including McNeil Island and Alcatraz.

During his ten years at Alcatraz, beginning in 1942, Quillen worked in many different jobs and even plotted escape, unsuccessfully. During the 1946 three-day siege, Quillen was in D Block isolation, which had been assaulted by exploding grenades, tear gas, and showering glass.

After seven years at Alcatraz, an unexpected visit from his father and stepmother turned his life around—because he now had someone who cared. Quillen took correspondence classes to earn credits toward his high school diploma and, because of his attitude change, had his good time restored. Soon thereafter he worked as an orderly in the hospital at Alcatraz, a field that he would continue in when he was released.

After serving ten years at Alcatraz, Quillen was transferred to McNeil Island for three years, where he took classes and expanded his hospital work. Quillen's next incarcerations were in San Quentin for one year and at a forestry camp in Humboldt County, California. He was released under a thirty-year parole in 1958. After his release, Quillen lived with his sister's family. He later married, held a career in radiology for twenty-five years, and received a presidential pardon in 1980 from President Jimmy Carter. Quillen died in 1998.

Thus, it was possible for a motivated inmate to reduce his sentence by 50 percent.

Freedom Dreams

Many inmates, however, had no incentive to earn time off for good behavior. Some were serving two or three lifetime sentences. Consequently, since their sentences were impossible to outlive, these prisoners embraced one goal: ESCAPE! Often escape plots were carefully planned, but sometimes the escape attempt was an act of hasty, mindless desperation. Jim Quillen explains his "freedom" urges:

I had been continually searching for anything that would give me a small chance to again be in the free world. I could never resign myself to serving thirty years in prison. I was young, full of life and energy and did not want to spend my life in prison. I knew my chances were slight to nonexistent, but I felt inside that somehow, some way, I had to try to escape.[76]

Quillen also says that "an escape attempt from [Alcatraz] was often a death sentence. . . . There was a feeling among the inmates that if one attempted to escape, he must be prepared to die."[77]

The unwritten policy among officers at Alcatraz was to kill prisoners attempting to escape. Most correctional officers enforced it. Inmates, however, felt that guards could have captured unarmed escapees without killing them.

The Battle of Alcatraz

Anger and frustration motivated the bloodiest siege on Alcatraz, known as the Battle of Alcatraz. The six men involved were so desperate that, rather than exist in Alcatraz, they were resolved to die if they did not break out. The escape attempt began on May 2, 1946, after the noon meal when most of the inmates were at work. The plan was to obtain firearms from the gun gallery, release the prisoner population into the yard, storm the guard towers and catwalks, and "take" Alcatraz.

During the three-day revolt, six inmates systematically overpowered a total of nine officers and locked them in two cells. Later, one convict opened fire on the captured men, injuring most of them. Marines and prison guards from San Quentin, McNeil Island, and Leavenworth were called in as reinforcements. By dropping nearly 150 grenades through ventilation shafts and into utility quarters, and shooting fiery rifle grenades into D Block windows, the chaos finally came under control.

Three of the six escapees—Marvin Hubbard, Bernard Coy, and Joe Cretzer—were found slain in the C Block utility corridor. The other three—Sam Shockley, Clarence Carnes, and Miran Thompson—aborted the escape attempt and returned to their cells after witnessing the shooting of the guards.

After being tried for the deaths of the two officers, Shockley and Thompson were executed in a gas chamber at San Quentin prison thirty-one months after the siege. Carnes avoided a death sentence (possibly because he showed mercy by refusing to slash the

Smoke billows from the cell block during the Battle of Alcatraz. Two officers and three prisoners died in the 1946 escape attempt.

necks of the captured officers who remained alive or because of his young age—nineteen years old); instead, a second life sentence was added to his time.

The gory battle left two officers and three prisoners dead and seventeen officers and one prisoner wounded. Several lessons emerged from the Alcatraz battle. Quillen, who happened to be locked in D Block, where the terrified inmates hid behind mattresses during the siege, lists two lessons:

> The inmates realized that there were no extremes the officials would not employ to insure the inescapability of the prison. Administration learned that there was a time when pettiness, degradation and humiliation must stop, or others (like Coy, Cretzer and Hubbard) would reach the point where life was no longer important.[78]

Prison administration acknowledged the insignificance of certain regulations (like but-toning the top button of one's shirt), and banned harassment of inmates over such petty rules.

An Unsolved Escape

Another escape attempt, on June 11, 1962, resulted in the mysterious and controversial escape of three inmates—mysterious, because the inmates' bodies were never found.

The three escapees—brothers Clarence and John Anglin and inmate Frank Morris—spent eleven months preparing for their escape. They used many supplies in the escape scheme, including paint from paint kits, hair from the barbershop, pulped and painted magazine pages (similar to papier-mâché) to make fake cardboard grilles, soap and concrete shavings to make dummy heads, more than fifty raincoats for makeshift life preservers and two rubber boats, and drills, files, and other tools. Fortunately for the escapees, they found helpful instructions on how to build inflatable pon-

The escapees placed dummy heads (left) in their beds at night so they could work undetected. At right, a guard examines the escape hole gouged by one of the prisoners.

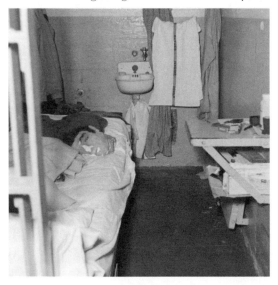

toons and vest floatation devices in *Sports Illustrated* and *Popular Mechanics,* which were obtained from the prison library.

Using spoons, the inmates gouged through the deteriorating cement surrounding the ten-by-six-inch ventilator holes in their cells, enlarging them to ten-by-eighteen-inches. For months, with lifelike dummy heads in their bunks to fool officers during nighttime counts, the convicts used the recessed area above the cells for a workshop and storage place. Using abrasive string, they also cut through the tool-proof bars that secured the ventilator shafts and led to the roof.

On the night of the escape, the men burrowed through the vents and into the utility corridor behind the rear cell walls. They then climbed a mass of pipes thirty feet to the roof and shinnied down a forty-foot drain pipe to the ground. After scaling a twelve-foot fence topped by barbed wire, they made their way to the water and disappeared forever.

A feverish hunt by air, land, and sea turned up no bodies. Days later, a floating oar was found and a plastic-wrapped pouch of sixty photos and names linked to the Anglins was discovered floating near some rocks at the foot of the Golden Gate Bridge. Authorities list the three inmates as drowned; however, others believe that the men may have been picked up by a prearranged boat, managed to escape the dragnet in the surrounding communities, and went on to find refuge outside the United States.

The almost thirty-year reputation of Alcatraz as an escape-proof prison had been tarnished. During Alcatraz's twenty-nine years of service as a federal maximum-security prison, there had been fourteen escape attempts involving thirty-four inmates. (Because two inmates, Shockley and Cretzer, were involved in two escape attempts, some books list the number as thirty-six.) Six inmates were assumed drowned—although only one body was recovered—and seven inmates were shot to death. The rest were recaptured.

After any escape attempts, other inmates never admitted knowledge of breakout plans when interviewed by the FBI and the prison administration. They did this for self-protection, to give hope to those hopelessly incarcerated, and to frustrate authorities.

Employee and Family Life on the Rock

Employees who lived on Alcatraz Island had different experiences than those who lived on the mainland. Those who lived on the island had a relatively normal and safe life considering they lived in close proximity to several hundreds of America's most dangerous criminals. The Rock's civilian population numbered over two hundred. The island had enough apartments and cottages to house about sixty families and rooms for about ten bachelors. Sometimes there would be as many as seventy-five children living within the small, close-knit community.

Some residents described Alcatraz as a peaceful place, even going so far as to call it a poor man's Hawaii. Jolene Babyak's father worked at Alcatraz penitentiary from 1953 through 1962. Part of that time, the family lived on the island, occupying either the so-called Sixty-four Building or the associate warden's Spanish-style duplex. Babyak shared fond memories of the island in her book *Eyewitness on Alcatraz*:

> Alcatraz was perhaps the most beautiful home I've ever had. On a breezy, crystal-clear day, the bay is a magical setting, with two bridges—one, the Golden Gate, perhaps the most famous bridge in the world—defining the perimeters of the dramatic skyline of San Francisco. The bay itself was breathtaking theatre. Ships slid under the Golden Gate past our island; pugged-nosed tug boats churned up the white caps. The waves were fre-quently dotted with boats and their glistening white, yawning sails.[79]

Even though the island housed vicious criminals, the wives and children of employees saw prisoners only from a distance. Parents said they felt safer living on Alcatraz Island than in San Francisco. There was no traffic, and home burglaries simply did not exist. Because of the locked gates and fences everywhere, security was not a problem. Parents primarily worried that their children would either fall into the bay and be carried away by the strong currents, fall down a steep cliff, or fall into the sea on their rocky boat rides to school in San Francisco.

Bachelor Quarters

About 50 percent of the staff lived on the island. Since San Francisco was expensive, there were advantages to living on Alcatraz beyond not having to commute. Correctional Officer Frank Heaney, a single man, shared his feelings about living on the island:

> Personally, I didn't mind the living conditions at all. I lived in the bachelor quarters of the converted military chapel. For $10 a month, I got a bed and bureau, and my laundry done. Either I ate the same food as the inmates, or I ate with one of the families on the island, or I went into San Francisco for meals.

There was a lot of recreation for us: bowling and billiards, dancing and card playing. There was a handball court that doubled as a gymnasium, a kid's playground, and places for picnicking, fishing, and crabbing. Female guests of single men were not allowed in our quarters; but our male friends and relatives could be entertained anywhere in the residential areas. And it was a big deal to be able to invite someone to visit you on Alcatraz. I never knew I had so many friends.[80]

Family Apartments

The first housing assigned to new families coming to Alcatraz was usually in the Sixty-four Building next to the wharf. The dreary three-story building, which was formerly army barracks, had been converted into twenty-seven apartments. The simple apartments had twelve-foot ceilings, uneven floors, and steam radiators. A canteen and post office were also housed in the building.

The newer apartments—in Buildings A, B, and C, located across the parade ground—had a waiting list. In 1947 Donald Hurley's family moved into the C building that had eighteen apartments. The three-bedroom apartments had pegged wood floors, stainless steel sinks, balconies, and spectacular views of San Francisco. The monthly rent of forty-seven dollars and fifty cents included laundry services.

The biggest inconvenience to families was the erratic and insufficient supply of electrical power. Alcatraz made its own electricity with a diesel-powered generator. The power supplied by the generator was direct current (DC) rather than the commonly used alternating current (AC). This DC caused common AC appliances such as toasters, vacuum cleaners, irons, and televisions to burn out instantly when they were turned on. Because of this problem, numerous families purchased converters to change the power from DC to AC. The chief of mechanical service warned everyone against

Sixty-four Building, where new families on Alcatraz were assigned to live. The building contained twenty-seven apartments, a post office, and a canteen.

Childhood Experiences on Alcatraz

In her book *Eyewitness on Alcatraz*, Jolene Babyak recalls her early impressions as a young girl living on the island.

"[One of] my first mixed recollections of Alcatraz at age seven [took place] at night, [hearing] the pitch and yaw of convicts on a vocal rampage. (They'd yell at times and drag their cups on the bars. Officer Bill Long later said they would often stage a welcoming party whenever new prisoners came on the island.) I remember asking about the noise as I was tucked into bed, and being reassured that it was just inmates, as we called them, letting off steam. Although my parents didn't communicate fear to me, or even hatred of prisoners, I knew to keep my distance, and that behavior generated a childlike feeling of awe and a hushed reverence, as if prisoners were special people. Special, but dangerous perhaps. I found them fascinating—but I kept my distance."

using converters because they drew too much power from the direct current system. But some renters smuggled converters in during the night.

One resident, Dick Waszak, installed his family's converter in the bathroom. Consequently, that is where his wife, Maryanne, used her electric appliances to prepare waffles and mashed potatoes. In addition, since Maryanne could not plug in her Amana freezer, she cleverly used it as a linen closet.

Because of the prisoners, discarding family trash was restricted. Since newspapers and some magazines were banned to the prisoners, they could not be dumped with the regular garbage and had to be disposed of separately. To keep certain items out of the hands of prisoners who had trash duty, families dumped cutlery, tools, bottles, glassware, and clothing into the bay.

Boat Transportation

When families first moved to the island, they soon discovered one of the problems with the twelve-minute boat ride to and from San Francisco: too few trips. In the early years, only seven or eight trips a day were scheduled. Because of their dissatisfaction, boat trips were later increased to eleven, and by the late 1950s, the boat made twenty-two round trips daily.

The first service boat was the *McDowell*, a fifty-foot launch with a seating capacity of about forty people. In 1945 a new boat constructed by McNeil Island prisoners began service. Named the *Warden Johnston*, this launch had a pilothouse, a private cabin, a main cabin for fifty people, and outside seating. In about 1960, this boat was replaced with the *Warden Madigan*, a broad-beamed, high-bowed cruiser that had been converted from a Korean War steel supply boat.

The changing tides, the gangplank, and floating platform all provided challenging situations in embarking and disembarking the boat. Sometimes passengers carrying packages or appliances lost their footing (and their dignity) while scrambling onto the bobbing boat. In 1959 a correctional officer and his son accidentally dropped a new eight-hundred-dollar color console television set into the swirling water while trying to board the *Warden Johnston*.

The School Timetable

Since all of the children on Alcatraz attended school in San Francisco, they adjusted their lives to the boat schedule. The school boat left at 7:20 A.M. for junior and senior high students and at 8:20 A.M. for the elementary school children. After-school boats returned students to Alcatraz at 3:30 P.M. and 4:10 P.M. Jolene Babyak recalls her school days:

> It was just like ants when the school boat whistle blew. Kids ran out of their apartments, across the big playground, down the steps by the side of 64 Building and across the balcony; they plowed down the steep, terraced, concrete stairway between the balcony and the Dock tower, hitting the dock about the same time as the boarding whistle blew.
>
> Most of us got pretty good at bouncing down those steps two and three at a time, while a silent and rather stern woman known as the "balcony lieutenant" watched daily from the railing of 64 Building to make sure none of us fell into the bay.[81]

When space became available, employee families moved to the newer apartments in Buildings A, B, and C.

After disembarking at the Fort Mason pier, children walked in groups to their schools, sometimes a mile away. Instead of Midwestern snow days, children at Alcatraz looked forward to days of high winds and rough waters, which allowed them to miss about five days of school a year.

The last scheduled boat trip to the island was at midnight. However, latecomers could request a 2:00 A.M. trip. If a teenager missed the midnight boat, he or she had two options: stay over in San Francisco or call the control center officer from the city to request the boat. Since most families did not have telephone connections to the city, the embarrassed teen had to call the control center officer who, in turn, notified the teen's parents. In the late 1940s two phone booths were installed from which employees could make calls off the island.

Children's Activities

Family activities were confined to a two-acre part of the island, most of them taking place on the windswept concrete parade ground. Four cottages, the associate warden's/captain's duplex, apartment buildings A, B, and C, a playground, and a recreation hall bordered the perimeter of the parade ground. Children used the large concrete slab for playing games such as touch football, baseball, tennis, and other activities that included flying kites, riding tricycles and bikes, and roller skating.

Former resident Joyce Rose Ritz recalls: "We were hot-shot roller skaters. We used to put up a pole and a [sheet] and the wind would catch, and you'd zip across [the parade ground] thirty miles an hour. About all the kids broke their bones at one time or another."[82]

Children from Alcatraz took a boat to and from school in San Francisco.

Living on the island from 1942 until 1953, Donald Hurley recalled the scary rides in orange crates down a fifty-step stairway. The tiny steps, which led from the parade ground to the canteen in the Sixty-four Building, were meant to cause a running escapee to trip and tumble. But to adventurous children, the steps served as an excellent speed ramp, even though the crate disintegrated upon impact at the bottom. In his book *Alcatraz Island Memories*, Hurley describes a game that he played as a child:

The most popular game we played was called "Guards and Cons." . . . We had the perfect prison, which was between an apartment and one of the island's natural rock walls. To the rear of this ten-foot-by-twenty-five-foot enclosed area, was a forty foot-high, chain-link fence. The guards had to stand behind a certain point. A con would start to climb the fence. If the guard could not get up to the fence fast enough to tag him, then there was an escape. The escaped con could only hide in 64 Building and once he found a place to hide he had to stay there. The guards (usually two for one escape) would have one half hour to find him. Of course, everyone wanted to be a con.[83]

Unexpected Communication with Prisoners

Babyak describes how she once had a face-to-face encounter with a prisoner:

We'd see prisoners working nearby, separated from us by a fence. Once, when I was eight, a prisoner found a hard rubber ball in the weeds and beckoned to me. I

A Halloween party on Alcatraz. The children also enjoyed roller skating and playing "guards and cons."

shyly approached, as the guard stood there, and the man pushed the ball through the fence to me. It was a proud moment: I had in my hand *the* most valued item on Alcatraz—the coveted black handball that had rolled down the hill from over the prison yard wall. And it had been given to me by a prisoner. It was my first "real life" conflict—whether to say thank you to an adult, or to not speak to a convict. I'm equally sure it was my first compromise. I may have said thanks, but he probably didn't hear it.[84]

Hurley remembered a Christmas Eve tradition on the island. Under the direction of an adult, all of the children went Christmas caroling throughout the residential areas beginning at the dock. The last stop was the restricted area up the hill to Warden Johnston's house for a party. About one hundred feet from the D Block exterior wall, the carolers stopped and sang a couple of songs and then shouted "Merry Christmas!" to the inmates. Inmates echoed their greetings back.

The wardens of Alcatraz lived in this 18 room residence.

Each year Hurley thought, "Our happiest night must have been one of their saddest."[85]

Other Recreation

Other activities took place in the recreation building, which had Ping-Pong and pool tables and a two-lane bowling alley. The building was the scene of family parties and teen dances. Teens could invite their friends to Alcatraz, but they had to escort them over on the boat. Because Alcatraz held an air of mystery and danger, most treasured the visit.

One benefit that the men working on Alcatraz appreciated was the abundant fishing. Sometimes the bass were so concentrated in the water that several guards could fish through the night and catch enough to feed the entire prison population.

Most routine activities, such as shopping trips and school attendance, required a trip by ferry. To guard against feelings of isolation, residents on the island formed social clubs for all ages. One example was the

Women's Club. In the 1950s they produced and sold cookbooks through *Sunset* magazine. Profits were used for children's activities and parties on the island. Family life for the employees was serene most of the time, but their working lives were not as predictable.

Employees

Employees on Alcatraz included the administrative personnel, Public Health Service staff, industry foremen, a lighthouse keeper (before automation in the 1950s), maintenance men, and a member of the Coast Guard.

During the twenty-nine year existence of Alcatraz as a federal penitentiary, there were four wardens: James A. Johnston (1934–1948), Edwin Swope (1948–1955), Paul J. Madigan (1955–1961), and finally Olin G. Blackwell, who served from 1961 until Alcatraz closed on March 21, 1963.

Wardens maintained discipline. And their testimony regarding an inmate's willingness to cooperate could ultimately affect a prisoner's

Wardens at Alcatraz

James A. Johnston: 1934–1948. Alcatraz prison became James A. Johnston's third assignment as a warden. The Bureau of Prisons, which considered Johnston a prison progressive, insisted that he uphold its intention that Alcatraz be renowned for its severe regulations and for housing the nation's most dangerous criminals. Setting the rules and tone of the prison, Johnston, sixty years old at the beginning of his assignment, kept up his revered reputation for sternness. Even though Johnston was well liked by both employees and prisoners, he enacted many stiff rules, one being silence, which some considered inhumane. Ten escape attempts occurred during his fourteen years as warden.

Edwin Swope: 1948–1955. Appointed from New Mexico State Penitentiary, Edwin Swope was militant and uncompromising with inmates and staff. Swope did not possess the refined style of Johnston. His patronizing manner toward employees caused their morale to plunge. When the culinary workers went on strike, he insisted that officers wait on tables. This not only lowered officer morale but also caused the inmates to lose respect for the guards. Swope further irked guards when he removed stools in the gun towers, reasoning that they would remain more alert by standing during their eight-hour shift. Swope returned the stools when the guards resisted the change.

Paul J. Madigan: 1955–1961. Paul J. Madigan was the most qualified person for the position of warden at Alcatraz. He held many positions at the prison, including guard, lieutenant, captain, and associate warden. His listening skills endeared him to both personnel and inmates. Convicts nicknamed Madigan "Promising Paul" because he promised to look into all of their concerns. Soon after Madigan became warden, he installed radio headphones in the cells. Beginning in 1957, Madigan brightened Christmas with cigars, chocolate candy, and a special Christmas menu. When Madigan was captain of the guards in 1941, his levelheadedness saved lives. Four escapees had bound up Madigan and several other officers in one of the industry buildings during a breakout attempt. When the escapees were unsuccessful in cutting the tool-resistant bars, Madigan convinced the frustrated inmates to give themselves up before the next count.

Olin G. Blackwell: 1961–1963. As the final warden of Alcatraz, Olin G. Blackwell inherited an aging, crumbling prison and served during a controversial period. The liberal, relaxed Blackwell wanted to continue the generous programs he had instigated as deputy warden, which had included installing hot water in the cells; adding new yard sports such as weight lifting, basketball, and volleyball; and allowing newscasts and talk shows on the inmates' radio stations. At age forty-six— one of the youngest wardens in the federal system— Blackwell favored relaxing the atmosphere at Alcatraz. That put him in the middle of the older, stricter guards and the incoming younger, more lenient guards. During the unsolved Anglin-Morris escape, Blackwell was on vacation. Although three towers had been closed down at the time, the soft-spoken Texan attributed all escapes to human failure.

chances before the parole board. The warden's assistants, known as associate or deputy wardens, administered necessary minor punishments. Associate wardens also allotted inmate work assignments, including industry jobs. Because wardens and associate wardens controlled the punishments, they were not popular with the prisoners.

Correctional officers had different problems. One of the most crucial was maintaining a delicate balance between humane treatment and the necessary display of authority. James V. Bennett succeeded Sanford Bates as director of the Bureau of Prisons in 1937. In his book *I Chose Prison*, Bennett explains the prison officer's first dilemma in how to associate with his charges:

> If [the officer] allows a prisoner to become aware of the compassion he feels, will he destroy his usefulness as an individual responsible for all the other prisoners? The prison officer, according to the manual of regulations, ought to remain impassive and fair.[86]

Guard Bill Rogers, who worked on Alcatraz during the years 1958–1963, said that the smart officers treated prisoners with fairness. "Either they respected you or they did not. If you were known as a guy who—in order to get back at an inmate—would bum-rap him or plant something on him, God help you if the inmates ever took over the cell house."[87]

Salary Enticements for Prison Officers

When Alcatraz opened in 1934, the United States was in the middle of the Great Depression—a time of great unemployment. The annual starting salary for a federal prison officer was $3,000 compared to a state prison officer, who started at $2,400. The attractive federal salary enticed many men, including those working in other prisons, to seek federal prison jobs.

In order to cover the three eight-hour work shifts at Alcatraz Federal Penitentiary, ninety officers were needed. In the early years, Alcatraz employed only the best and the

In the 1950s, the guards being hired were younger and less experienced than ever before. To prepare for their work, they practiced wrestling, jujitsu, and role-playing.

Guard Frank Heaney describes in his book *Inside the Walls of Alcatraz* how the inmates harassed guards during counts.

"Inmates were required to stand in front of their cells while we walked down the tiers and counted them. They were required to stand at attention; the only time they didn't have to was if they had to urinate or have a bowel movement. Then they could sit on or stand in front of the toilet.

Coincidentally, it seemed that's what they would be doing most often. They'd sit or stand grinning at me while they exhibited themselves. I knew they were trying to get to me psychologically, and I didn't want to lose control; so I would concentrate on being highly involved with the counts.

The more I tried to ignore them, the cruder they became, until I was forced to threaten to put them on report. Most of the time that put a stop to it—for a while—but then it would start up all over again. Little things like that could get to you after a while. Those kinds of subtle harassments sent many a guard over the edge."

most experienced men in the bureau. In the 1950s high unemployment again created job interest for correctional officer positions. By 1959 the beginning salary had risen to $4,480 a year (which amounted to $2.15 per hour). But at this time, the guards being hired were younger and were not always experienced.

Author Marilyn Tower Oliver reviewed the training and schooling of potential guards, also known as correctional officers:

The guards had to go through a demanding training course that included gymnastics, marching, drilling, boxing, wrestling, jujitsu, and the use of weapons such as gas and firearms. They were also trained in sociology, psychology, and criminology to help them understand the criminal mind. They took part in role-playing exercises to teach them how to react in dealing with inmates.[88]

The Youngest Guard

Frank Heaney was the youngest (and least-experienced) guard ever to serve at Alcatraz prison. In March 1947 twenty-year-old Heaney saw the employment listing for an Alcatraz correctional officer tacked up on a post office wall. Heaney later recalled his first interview:

When I was being interviewed, the warden spent an hour and a half trying to convince me not to go to work on Alcatraz. That was Warden Swope, a very stoic kind of guy. He wore a big stetson [hat] and glasses, and he stared right at you like he wanted to make sure you knew who was boss. He might have smiled once in his lifetime; maybe not that much. But then, there weren't too many smiles on Alcatraz.

Warden Swope asked me why in the world I wanted this job. . . . He got into the fact of my being so young: "Young man, you are absolutely too young and immature for this job. We need older seasoned men. It will just be too difficult for you." And he didn't let up for a long time.

Eventually though, he relented. I guess I reached his conscience when I said that I had taken the examination in good faith, that I had scored quite high on the civil service test, and that I thought I at least deserved a chance. At any rate, he hired me.[89]

Guard Patrols

As Warden Swope warned, being a correctional officer was a difficult job. To control security, guards had to keep inmates under continual observance. Six officers patrolled the three tiers in B and C Blocks, one on each tier. They varied their routines as much as possible to lessen the opportunities for the inmates to escape.

The most boring and least-liked job assignment was tower patrol. Working the towers was one of the jobs given to new officers or to men who had trouble working closely with prisoners. The job assignment lasted three to six months. Guard Frank Heaney tells how he felt about tower duty:

I hated working the towers. God, it was monotonous, particularly the midnight [to] 8:00 A.M. shift. It seemed like it was always bitter cold, with chilling winds every night. You couldn't really relax for a moment. Every so often a patrolling lieutenant would signal with a flashlight. If I hadn't signaled back with three flashes, I would have been fired.

I sneaked a radio up to the tower in my lunch bag once and played it real low. But the control center had loud speakers and the music was overheard. The fellow in charge up there told me one morning, "I know you got a radio. Get rid of it." If he had reported me, I would have been suspended for five days. For sleeping on duty, you got fired.[90]

Armed Posts

Guards were armed at three locations: the gun galleries, the yard wall posts, and the towers. There were six towers at Alcatraz. Weapons and equipment in each of the six towers consisted of a submachine gun, a rifle, a pistol, grenades, gas projectiles, searchlights, field glasses, and a telephone. Three towers—the dock, the road, and the main tower—were manned twenty-four hours a day.

The principal post was the three-story tall dock tower. Through the shatterproof glass, an officer could see the dock, the Sixty-four Building, the north cell house wall, the yard wall, the kitchen cage, the water tank, and the

Former guard Frank Heaney stands next to the guard tower in which he used to work.

hill tower. The dock tower officer also managed the key to the boat engine. He lowered the boxed key on a wire down to the boat pilot at the dock when it was requested. When the boat returned to Alcatraz, the boxed key was cranked back up to the tower. The tower guard kept a log noting the time and the officer who received the key in his book.

The second most important post was the road, or number two, tower. The officer stood with his back to San Francisco, facing the southeast side of the prison, the yard, its posts, and the stairway that prisoners used on their way to the industries. The third twenty-four-hour manned tower was the main tower, which was perched on top of the cell house.

The last three towers—the power house, hill, and model roof towers—overlooked the industries area and were manned only during daylight hours when inmates were out of their cells.

Other Watches

One officer patrolled the island at night with a flashlight searching for trespassers. The sounds of the surf, seagulls, rats, and yelping sea lions sometimes spooked the patrolling guards. Fog and cold weather also made the job unpleasant.

Armed guards also watched the inmates from gun galleries called cages. Cages were separately manned at varied times. For example, while the prisoners ate, the hill tower guard staffed the enclosed exterior dining room cage/catwalk, which ran the length of the room. And the kitchen cage, located behind the cell house, was manned when the culinary prisoners (cooks) were at work. When prisoners were in the yard, officers manned three corner gun cages that were connected by catwalks perched atop the yard walls. The yard-wall guards were armed with a pistol and a submachine gun.

Another area, the control room, was manned twenty-four hours a day. Considered the nerve center of Alcatraz, the room was protected from floor to waist height by three-eighths-inch steel and from waist height to the ceiling by one-and-a-half-inch bulletproof glass. A panel of instruments such as telephones, loudspeakers, fire alarms, and an island-wide emergency siren allowed communication with prisoners and with guards on duty in any part of the prison. A board of numbered keys for every door, shop, and gate hung on the wall. A sizable stock of rifles, revolvers, shotguns, hand grenades, tear gas, ammunition, and billy clubs completed the security system.

Even with all of the security precautions, some prisoners were successful in escaping. The two 1962 escape events were blamed mostly on the aging of the prison. But Alcatraz Federal Penitentiary would have to close for countless other reasons.

CHAPTER 8

Closing Alcatraz Prison: The Island's Future Roles

When Alcatraz lost its reputation as an escape-proof prison, the U.S. government conducted an investigation to determine whether it was worthwhile to keep the prison open. The rigid program originally implemented by Warden Johnston had been steadily relaxed during the administrations of the three succeeding wardens. Throughout the prison's twenty-nine years, rules for inmates had progressed from demanding strict silence to allowing oil painting and listening to approved radio stations. Many wondered if the Alcatraz maximum-security prison was now any different from other maximum-security federal prisons. Since the gangster era had ended, many penologists questioned the prison's necessity. Because numerous problems faced the penitentiary, its demise appeared inevitable.

Replacing Alcatraz

Because times had changed and national crime had decreased after World War II, some critics thought Alcatraz was no longer needed. By the late 1940s work camps and other low-security prisons were opening all over the country. Alcatraz seemed increasingly antiquated to James V. Bennett, director of the Bureau of Prisons. But men such as the Cretzers and Coys (the ruthless escapees in the 1946 Alcatraz takeover) could not intermix with mainland prisoners, and there was no other place except Alcatraz. In

1946 Bennett testified during congressional hearings regarding the Department of Justice appropriations. He suggested that a new maximum-custody prison must be built:

> Alcatraz serves a very worthwhile purpose in taking out of the other federal institutions the prisoners who, if they were permitted to remain, would make necessary a much more repressive program and complicate rehabilitative opportunities. The really bad apples must be taken out of the barrel.[91]

A portion of the deteriorating yard is seen here through the corroding bars of a window.

Are Criminals Born That Way

In his book *I Chose Prison*, James V. Bennett relates his opinion about why a person is a criminal and how to classify that person.

"Most American criminologists now hold there is no such animal as a born criminal, whose tendencies are inherited, inevitable, and not responsive to reform. Each criminal is now regarded as an individual problem. His case must be carefully studied with reference to heredity, environment, personality, and known behavior. There is a general inclination to deny that criminals may be rigorously classified, except on the basis of such formal data as criminal record, repetitions of types of crime, seriousness of crimes, and so on. It appears that no universal or single explanation of criminality is valid."

Bernard Coy, one of the attempted escapees of the May 2, 1946 Battle of Alcatraz.

Thus, until congress appropriated funds and built a new prison, the only alternative for the incorrigibles was Alcatraz. At the time, no one could have predicted that Alcatraz would remain open another seventeen years.

Excessive Costs

Called a prison experiment by penologists, Alcatraz penitentiary carried a high price tag. By the 1960s Bennett conceded that Alcatraz was "an administrative monstrosity."[92] Because Alcatraz was an island, all water, food, and other supplies had to be barged in. It became the most expensive penitentiary to operate in the federal system. Bennett told Wallace Turner of the *New York Times*, "The cost as of June 1962 was running $13.79 a day to keep a prisoner on Alcatraz, compared to a daily average of $5.37 in other federal prisons."[93]

Almost a decade earlier, even higher estimates were enumerated. When Senator William Langer—an adversary of the Alcatraz concept—last visited the prison in 1953, he told the Senate,

Alcatraz convicts could be boarded cheaper at the Waldorf-Astoria. The island prison was then costing approximately $5,000,000 a year to operate and "on my last inspection trip, it had only 150 inmates." This would average $33,333.33 a year per prisoner, or slightly more than $91 a day.[94]

The prison's deteriorating buildings posed another problem. Interestingly, the one thing that created security for Alcatraz—the surrounding saltwater—also caused the erosion of the prison. The cell house, steel towers, and other structures on the island had been absorbing the spraying saltwater, which caused the cement to break down and the steel to weaken from corrosion. An additional problem concerned sewage. Area residents concerned about the environment demanded that dumping sewage into the bay be stopped. But it would cost $5 million—almost twenty times the cost of the original remodeling in 1933—to repair the crumbling fixtures and alter sewage lines.

Besides the prison's tangible problems, author Don DeNevi lists a combination of other factors that were considered when closing Alcatraz:

> The increase in assaults and other types of violence; the turnover of officer personnel; the increase in the number of inexperienced officers; the general drop in officer morale; the pressure from a public concerned about the location of the prison; [and] the pressure from critical penologists.[95]

Consequently, Attorney General Robert F. Kennedy ordered the Rock closed in late 1962. To replace it, the Bureau of Prisons built a new $10-million maximum-security prison near Marion, Illinois. Unlike at Alcatraz, Kennedy announced that rehabilitation would be a factor at this prison: "Let us reject the spirit of retribution and attempt coolly to balance the needs of deterrent and detention with the possibilities of rehabilitation."[96]

Press Relations

Members of the press were never welcome at Alcatraz, making it next to impossible to obtain news. When Attorney General Kennedy held a news conference in San Francisco several months after the June 11, 1962, Morris-Anglin breakout, a reporter asked,

> Sir, the Department of Justice apparently has competent people out here but why, when anything happens at Alcatraz, are they voiceless? At such times, why is it necessary for newspapers to go to the trouble and expense day after day of calling Washington to check out tips or other information? Have you, Sir, any proposals for correcting this problem?

Attorney General Robert F. Kennedy ordered Alcatraz closed in 1962.

Prisoners board a boat to leave Alcatraz and relocate to other prisons.

The young attorney general grinned. "Call collect."[97]

But this attitude only added fuel to the fires of controversy. Alcatraz had a reputation for medieval cruelty and inflexible discipline. Authorities at other prisons said that Alcatraz's secret operating methods shielded management from criticism and could lead to mistreatment of prisoners. Because the press was not allowed on the island, the only way to learn about the prison's treatment of inmates came from relocated convicts. And possibly, transferring inmates fed reporters exaggerated stories of abuse.

Vacating the Prison

In the fall of 1962, authorities began to relocate Alcatraz inmates to other prisons, including Leavenworth in Kansas, Atlanta in Georgia, and Terre Haute in Indiana. Since Terre Haute was a medium-security prison, this suggests that not all prisoners incarcerated at Alcatraz were the nation's most hardened criminals.

The last prisoner to arrive at Alcatraz was Frank C. Weatherman—assigned number 1576—in December 1962. Weatherman was also the final convict to leave on the morning of March 21, 1963. That morning after breakfast, officers issued fresh prison blues and new pea coats to the last twenty-seven inmates. When cell doors opened for the last time, officers placed the men in handcuffs, leg irons, and waist chains and escorted them single file down Broadway. A launch chugged the inmates across the bay. From the pier, trains transported the prisoners to different penitentiaries.

After the remaining inmates left the island, the property was turned over to the General Services Administration (GSA), which handled surplus government property. Two caretakers maintained the empty island. Over the next several years, suggestions for new uses of the property poured in from everywhere. The ideas—including a western Statue of Liberty, a nudist colony, a casino, and a park commemorating the U.S. space program—were all rejected for various reasons.

To understand the motives of the Native Americans in claiming Alcatraz, it is important to know why they wanted some land to call their own. Native Americans have long felt persecuted because of their great land losses to the U.S. government. These losses have amounted to 95 percent of their holdings since 1800. Cherokee Wilma Mankiller shares her opinion in Troy R. Johnson's *We Hold the Rock*:

"Immediately following the Indian War Era, there began a series of government policies that were designed to make sure that we didn't exist anymore as tribal people. That we no longer had our language, our cultural identity, our religion, and most importantly, our land and natural resources."

Landings on Alcatraz

A year after the penitentiary closed, Native Americans claimed Alcatraz Island as Indian land. They made three landings before they officially occupied the island. The first—a four-hour stay—in March 1964, involved five Sioux Indians sailing to Alcatraz and signing a land claim under an 1868 Sioux treaty that entitled them to take possession of government surplus land. They wished to use the property for an Indian cultural center and university, spiritual and ecology centers, and a museum. Presidential commission hearings failed to act on their proposals, however.

After five years of waiting for an answer from the commission, the Native Americans forged ahead on a plan of action. The only way to awaken the American public's attention to their plight was through activism and occupation of government property. LaNada Boyer, of the Shoshone-Bannock tribe, recalls, "It was like we were an invisible people. They recognized everyone else, but they never recognized the Indian people—it was like we were part of a museum."[98]

On November 9, 1969, about seventy-five people assembled at San Francisco's Pier Thirty-nine. San Francisco State College student Richard Oakes of the Mohawk tribe, read a proclamation to the media offering twenty-four dollars in glass beads and red cloth for the island. (That is what the Dutch colonists paid the Indians for Manhattan Island in 1626.) Calling themselves "Indians of All Tribes," a group of five, and later another group of twenty, landed on Alcatraz that day, but all were peaceably escorted off by the Coast Guard the next morning.

Not giving up, the group made a third attempt. On November 20 about eighty Native Americans, consisting of college students, married couples, and six children, landed— this time prepared to stay and endure sacrifice and hardship. As John Trudell, a member of the Sioux tribe, explains,

The occupation of Alcatraz was in reality an issue of law. The American Government signed 300 [to] 400 treaties with different native tribes in this country. We were taking the legal position . . . saying to the American Government and the American people that your government must obey that law.[99]

Boyer describes the experience: "It was a wonderful feeling when we arrived. We got off the boat and we were all there together as a united group. We were going to make a stand and we were doing it on behalf of our people."[100]

Establishing a New Life

The group set up their headquarters in the abandoned three-story warden's residence. They used the cell house for living quarters and the industry buildings for secure hiding places should government officials attempt to remove them. The government, under President Richard Nixon, considered forcibly removing the new visitors, but due to growing public support for the Indians, decided against a raid.

Within three weeks, the group created a council. The council set up rules, installed a security system, formed an elementary school for twelve students, and addressed health and childcare issues. San Franciscans saw their bonfires and sometimes heard the sounds of their chanting.

A public relations office on the island managed sightseers, journalists, and photographers. As days turned into months, many activities—transmitting radio broadcasts; publishing a nationally distributed newsletter; handling donations of food, supplies, and money; receiving new arrivals, and considering proposals and counterproposals—kept the inhabitants busy.

Power Struggles

Federal officials refused to hold discussions with the Native Americans unless they left the island. But the tribes felt they gained more

Native Americans occupied the island of Alcatraz continuously from November 20, 1969 to June 11, 1971.

A 1953 congressional relocation program that moved the Native Americans from their reservations to large cities was flawed with hollow promises of vocational training, financial assistance, job placement, and housing. In Troy R. Johnson's book *We Hold the Rock*, two women tell of the betrayal. Millie Ketcheshawno of the Mvskoke Creek tribe tells about her relocation experience.

"About eight of us went by train from Kansas to the Bay Area. The BIA [Bureau of Indian Affairs] people told us they were going to meet us at the train station, but when we arrived in Oakland . . . nobody was there to meet us and we didn't know what to do. So we took a taxi downtown. Luckily, there was somebody in the office and they made arrangements for us to stay somewhere and told us to come back the next morning. We sat there in those offices for days on end with nothing to do, waiting to be sent out on interviews."

LaNada Boyer of the Shoshone-Bannock tribe recalls, "I saw signs that said 'No Indians or Dogs Allowed.' I remember the bathrooms for Indians only. And I remember the treatment of people towards us." Left stranded, impoverished, and subjected to prejudice for years, the American Indians established the United Native Americans organization in 1968 to unify all persons of Indian blood.

bargaining strength by remaining on the island. However, on December 4 problems began: all power went out on the island—the generators were inoperative, food spoiled, the GSA disconnected telephone lines, and water and fuel lines leaked. Also, resentments among leaders were causing friction. Ed Castillo of the Cahuillo-Luiseño tribe later, said, "Indian politics are just like everybody else's politics. There were a lot of different ideas on who was going to be in charge and who was going to make the rules and be exempt from the rules."[101]

On January 3, 1970, Richard Oakes's daughter died in a fall on the island. A few days later, the Oakes family departed Alcatraz, leaving a void in leadership. The focus of the island occupation was lost, and a power struggle for political control led to the tribes' downfall. The next several months led to meetings with government officials. However, the Native Americans rejected all proposals, insisting on money and a title to Alcatraz Island. The government would not agree to that.

On June 1, 1970, at 11:00 P.M., a string of fires gutted several historic buildings including the lighthouse, the warden's house, and the recreation hall. As Trudell explains,

> They [the American Government] wanted to incorporate it [Alcatraz] into the park system. They had taken our water. And then the fire happened. And it will never be known who started the fire. It could have been their side, it could have been our side, it could have been both sides.[102]

Public support for the Native Americans eroded. Less than thirty people remained on the island, holding out for another year. Then, on June 11, 1971, armed U.S. marshals, GSA security personnel, and FBI agents led the last fifteen people off the island. The Native Americans' occupation had lasted nineteen months and nine days.

Island Control Changes

During the next sixteen months, the GSA continued its administration of Alcatraz Island. To prevent anyone else from occupying the island, crews from the GSA began bulldozing buildings into rubble piles. The razing included the residential apartment complex, cottages, and a duplex where penitentiary employees and their families had lived.

In 1972 Congress created the Golden Gate National Recreation Area (GGNRA), a national park that started at thirty-four thousand acres but by the year 2000 had grown to about seventy-four thousand acres. The GGNRA included Alcatraz, and the island came under the administration of the National Park Service (NPS).

The NPS began offering public tours of the island in October 1973. Officials at the NPS were vastly surprised at the public interest. By the year 2000, annual visitors numbered over 1.3 million. Ferries carry visitors from San Francisco's Pier Forty-one to Alcatraz. After the ten-minute boat trip, the NPS provides cell house tours, a movie, and informative ranger talks highlighting the history of the island.

Fires during the Indian occupation destroyed several of Alcatraz's buildings. Here, tourists inspect some of the ruins on Alcatraz.

The unfolding history of Alcatraz Island came full circle. It began with birds as its inhabitants, then soldiers, prisoners and

A seagull perches atop a piece of rubble in front of Alcatraz's lighthouse.

guards, and now it has, for the most part, been returned to the birds. Today, nature has reclaimed the island. Besides allowing visitors to view history, it is a protected haven for endangered birds and flowering plants. During mating and birthing seasons (February through August on Alcatraz), many nature trails are off-limits to visitors.

The absence of four-footed predators made the island a haven for thousands of pelicans, gulls, cormorants, and other seabirds, which originally had the island to themselves before the mid-1800s' military development. The military blasting of cliff rocks forced the birds to move elsewhere along the San Francisco coastline. But the fallen boulders created shoreline tide pools for thriving populations of crabs, sea stars, and other marine animals that provided a diet for the handful of seagulls that floated in the air currents and squawked loudly during its prison years.

The primary birds on Alcatraz are the black-crowned night herons and the western gulls, but endangered brown pelicans and peregrine falcons also inhabit the island. With close observation, fluffy gull chicks can be seen near nesting sites on prison catwalks and atop guard towers.

Besides viewing a three-tiered collection of empty human cages, Alcatraz tourists may also encounter "living history." A visitor could meet a former correctional officer, a former island resident, or even a former prisoner. With the passage of decades came the healing of wounds and now both former guards and former prisoners can be friends. Nathan Glenn Williams, a former inmate, and now the author of *From Alcatraz to the White House,*

says he no longer fears his former guards, but he also admits that

> There was a time when I would have killed any one of them in an instant. We [had] such different perspectives. They went home, had a drink, and got to enjoy their families, while us convicts were locked in a small cell. But some of those men are now my closest friends. They eat dinner at my

house, and stay the night. Way back when, I'd have never dreamed of such a thing.[103]

For those unable to visit the island, the NPS has developed an Internet website (www.nps.gov/alcatraz) showing a selection of slides that cover the military years, prison life, the Indian occupation, nature on the island, and other related topics. The NPS has also preserved portions of the island to protect both its man-made and its natural features for the original inhabitants—birds. Eighty percent of the island is off-limits to the public due to safety hazards and for the protection of the winged population—over one hundred species of birds.

Visitors can also see flourishing gardens, left over from the military era and from prison employee families. About fifteen species of flowers, succulents, shrubs, and trees thrive on the island. They include the California poppy, ice plant, geraniums, and eucalyptus. A few land creatures on the island are deer mice, banana slugs, and the California slender salamander.

The Value of Alcatraz

But most visitors to Alcatraz Island are not there to see nature. It is the infamous prison that captures their interest. Long off-limits to the public, it is a curiosity because it is the only former federal prison open for tours.

The public, prison administrators, and penologists have questioned whether the se-vere environment and deprivation experienced at Alcatraz had been appropriate. The closing of the prison signaled the beginning of a new era of rehabilitation. Out of this new philosophy came the Marion penitentiary. It, too, was a trial and a new beginning for handling the incorrigibles.

After ten years, the prison at Marion, Illinois, had to reorganize. The hard-core prisoners had corrupted their new environment. A small percentage of men (about 1 percent) still needed to be isolated. One area at Marion is specified for these men and has tightened security. The violent men in these areas are even handcuffed before they leave their cells.

Former officer Frank Heaney later gave his opinion of Alcatraz:

I believe there is a definite need for a place like Alcatraz. It should be used only as a last resort, but always for that small group of violent and extreme offenders who violate—and will continue to harm their fellow human beings . . . even while they're behind bars.

In many ways, life inside a prison is the same as life on the outside. There will always be that small group who, for whatever the reason, will continue to break the rules and take advantage of others.

It is my belief—and I was there—that our only solution, our only *protection*, is truly to isolate them.[104]

Notes

Introduction: Criminals Must Be Separated from Society

1. Jim Quillen, *Alcatraz from Inside*. San Francisco: Golden Gate National Parks Association, 1991, p. viii.
2. Toby J. McIntosh, "Tourists on 'the Rock,'" *Progressive*, March 1975, p. 32.

Chapter 1: A Tough Prison for Tough Criminals

3. Quoted in James V. Bennett, *I Chose Prison*. New York: Alfred A. Knopf, 1970, p. 33.
4. Bennett, *I Chose Prison*, p. 32.
5. Frank Heaney and Gay Machado, *Inside the Walls of Alcatraz*. Palo Alto, CA: Bull, 1987, p. 19.
6. Sanford Bates, "The Battle Against Crime," 1999. www.notfrisco.com/alcatraz/BOP/Crime33.html.
7. Quoted in *Survey*, "Is It a Devil's Island?" November 1933, p. 383.
8. Quoted in *Survey*, "Is It a Devil's Island?" p. 383.
9. Philip O'Farrell, "Alcatraz Prison," *Survey*, January 1934, p. 30.
10. Department of Justice, "A New Prison," *Alcatraz: The Warden Johnston Years*, November 6, 1933. www.alsirat.com/alcatraz/documents/openpr.html.
11. Quoted in Michael A. Green, "The Mad Science of Alcatraz," 1998. http://members.aol.com/Beggar21/alcatraz.html.
12. Quoted in Don DeNevi, *Riddle of the Rock*. Buffalo, NY: Prometheus Books, 1991, pp. 22–23.
13. Quoted in DeNevi, *Riddle of the Rock*, p. 23.
14. Bennett, *I Chose Prison*, p. 11.
15. Quoted in Jolene Babyak, *Eyewitness on Alcatraz*. Berkeley, CA: Ariel Vamp, 1988, p. 10.
16. Quoted in Michael A. Green, "The Revolutionizing Impact of Johnston's Penology," 1998. http://members.aol.com/Beggar21/johnston.html.
17. Quoted in Joel Gazis-Sax, "American Siberia: The Purpose of Alcatraz," 1997. www.alsirat.com/alcatraz/purpose.html.
18. Quoted in Gazis-Sax, "American Siberia."
19. Edwin H. Sutherland, "America's Devil's Island," *Saturday Review of Literature*, September 10, 1949, p. 13.

Chapter 2: Arriving on the Rock: A Life Like No Other

20. Sutherland, "America's Devil's Island," p. 13.
21. Frederick R. Bechdolt, "The Rock," *Saturday Evening Post*, November 2, 1935, p. 5.
22. Howard Needham and Ted Needham, *Alcatraz*. Millbrae, CA: Celestial Arts, 1976, p. 19.
23. Alvin Karpis and Robert Livesey, *On the Rock*. New York: Beaufort Books, 1980, pp. 27–29.
24. Karpis and Livesey, *On the Rock*, p. 30.
25. Leon "Whitey" Thompson, *Last

Train to Alcatraz. Fiddletown, CA: Leon W. Thompson, 1988, p. 111.

26. Quoted in Heaney and Machado, *Inside the Walls of Alcatraz*, p. 33.
27. Quoted in Karpis and Livesey, *On the Rock*, p. 30.
28. Bechdolt, "The Rock," p. 6.
29. Quoted in Jay Stuller, "There Never Was a Harder Place than 'the Rock,'" *Smithsonian*, September 1995, p. 87.
30. Thompson, *Last Train to Alcatraz*, p. 150.
31. Quoted in Stuller, "There Never Was a Harder Place than 'the Rock,'" p. 87.
32. Quoted in Karpis and Livesey, *On the Rock*, p. 33.
33. Paul J. Madigan, *Institution Rules and Regulations*. San Francisco: Golden Gate National Parks Association, 1983, p. 1.
34. Madigan, *Institution Rules and Regulations*, p. 10.
35. Heaney and Machado, *Inside the Walls of Alcatraz*, p. 47.
36. Quoted in Thompson, *Last Train to Alcatraz*, p. 165.
37. Quoted in Thompson, *Last Train to Alcatraz*, p. 167.

Chapter 3: The Cell House

38. Karpis and Livesey, *On the Rock*, pp. 34–35.
39. Karpis and Livesey, *On the Rock*, p. 89.
40. Quillen, *Alcatraz from Inside*, p. 55.
41. Karpis and Livesey, *On the Rock*, pp. 237, 239.
42. Quillen, *Alcatraz from Inside*, p. 55.
43. Heaney and Machado, *Inside the Walls of Alcatraz*, p. 42.
44. Quillen, *Alcatraz from Inside*, p. 75.

45. Quillen, *Alcatraz from Inside*, p. 75.
46. Quillen, *Alcatraz from Inside*, p. 55.
47. Quillen, *Alcatraz from Inside*, pp. 76-77.
48. Karpis and Livesey, *On the Rock*, p. 77.
49. Heaney and Machado, *Inside the Walls of Alcatraz*, p. 79.

Chapter 4: Routine, Routine, Routine

50. Quillen, *Alcatraz from Inside*, p. 58.
51. Karpis and Livesey, *On the Rock*, p. 91.
52. Karpis and Livesey, *On the Rock*, pp. 52–53.
53. Quillen, *Alcatraz from Inside*, p. 52.
54. Quillen, *Alcatraz from Inside*, pp. 52–53.
55. Quoted in Needham and Needham, *Alcatraz*, p. 38.
56. Quillen, *Alcatraz from Inside*, p. 63.
57. J. Campbell Bruce, *Escape from Alcatraz*. New York: McGraw-Hill, 1963, pp. 106-107.
58. Karpis and Livesey, *On the Rock*, p. 123.
59. Bruce, *Escape from Alcatraz*, p. 48.

Chapter 5: Inmates' Leisure Time: Life by the Book

60. Heaney and Machado, *Inside the Walls of Alcatraz*, p. 52.
61. Quoted in Michael A. Green, "Privileges," 1998. http://members.aol.com/Beggar21/privilege.html.
62. Karpis and Livesey, *On the Rock*, pp. 50–51.
63. Quillen, *Alcatraz from Inside*, p. 61.
64. DeNevi, *Riddle of the Rock*, p. 99.
65. Donald J. Hurley, *Alcatraz Island Memories*. Sonoma, CA: Fog Bell Enterprises, 1987, p. 15.
66. Quillen, *Alcatraz from Inside*, p. 127.

67. Marilyn Tower Oliver, *Alcatraz Prison in American History*, Springfield, NJ: Enslow, 1998, p. 53.
68. Karpis and Livesey, *On the Rock*, p. 133.

Chapter 6: Breaking Prison Rules

69. Heaney and Machado, *Inside the Walls of Alcatraz*, p. 99.
70. Quoted in Bruce, *Escape from Alcatraz*, p. 50.
71. Bruce, *Escape from Alcatraz*, p. 49.
72. Karpis and Livesey, *On the Rock*, p. 230.
73. Karpis and Livesey, *On the Rock*, pp. 232–34.
74. Quillen, *Alcatraz from Inside*, p. 53.
75. Quoted in Babyak, *Eyewitness on Alcatraz*, pp. 42–43.
76. Quillen, *Alcatraz from Inside*, p. 64.
77. Quillen, *Alcatraz from Inside*, p. 56.
78. Quillen, *Alcatraz from Inside*, p. 123.

Chapter 7: Employee and Family Life on the Rock

79. Babyak, *Eyewitness on Alcatraz*, p. 4.
80. Heaney and Machado, *Inside the Walls of Alcatraz*, p. 64.
81. Babyak, *Eyewitness on Alcatraz*, p. 45.
82. Quoted in Babyak, *Eyewitness on Alcatraz*, p. 16.
83. Hurley, *Alcatraz Island Memories*, p. 75.
84. Babyak, *Eyewitness on Alcatraz*, p. 18.
85. Hurley, *Alcatraz Island Memories*, p. 72.
86. Bennett, *I Chose Prison*, p. 22.
87. Quoted in Babyak, *Eyewitness on Alcatraz*, p. 38.
88. Oliver, *Alcatraz Prison in American History*, p. 56.
89. Heaney and Machado, *Inside the Walls of Alcatraz*, p. 29.
90. Heaney and Machado, *Inside the Walls of Alcatraz*, p. 70.

Chapter 8: Closing Alcatraz Prison: The Island's Future Roles

91. Bennett, *I Chose Prison*, p. 113.
92. Quoted in Bruce, *Escape from Alcatraz*, p. 241.
93. Quoted in Bruce, *Escape From Alcatraz*, p. 237.
94. Bruce, *Escape from Alcatraz*, p. 238.
95. Don DeNevi, *Alcatraz '46*. San Rafael, CA: Leswing, 1974, p. 238.
96. Quoted in James Fuller, *Alcatraz Federal Penitentiary 1934-1963*. San Francisco: Asteron Production, 1982, p. 43.
97. Quoted in Bruce, *Escape from Alcatraz*, p. 237.
98. Quoted in Troy R. Johnson, *We Hold the Rock: The Indian Occupation of Alcatraz, 1969 to 1971*. San Francisco: Golden Gate National Parks Association, 1997, p. 11.
99. Quoted in Johnson, *We Hold the Rock*, p. 19.
100. Quoted in Johnson, *We Hold the Rock*, p. 22.
101. Quoted in Johnson, *We Hold the Rock*, p. 37.
102. Quoted in Johnson, *We Hold the Rock*, p. 42.
103. Quoted in Jay Stuller, *Alcatraz, the Prison*. San Francisco: Golden Gate National Parks Association, 1998, p. 39.
104. Heaney and Livesey, *Inside the Walls of Alcatraz*, p. 126.

For Further Reading

Books

Jolene Babyak, *Eyewitness on Alcatraz*. Berkeley, CA: Ariel Vamp, 1988. The daughter of an associate warden, Babyak tells a compelling story about life on Alcatraz through interviews with officers, other residents, and former inmates.

James Fuller, *Alcatraz Federal Penitentiary, 1934–1963*. San Francisco: Asteron Production, 1982. This forty-four-page paperback briefly presents the history and daily routine of Alcatraz along with short biographies of five famous prisoners and a description of the fourteen escape attempts.

Frank Heaney and Guy Machado, *Inside the Walls of Alcatraz*. Palo Alto, CA: Bull, 1987. The youngest guard ever to work in Alcatraz Federal Penitentiary, Heaney gives a first hand account of "The Rock."

Donald J. Hurley, *Alcatraz Island Memories*. Sonoma, CA: Fog Bell Enterprises, 1987. In this autobiography, Hurley describes his childhood experiences on Alcatraz while his father served as a correctional officer for eleven years (1942–1953).

Troy R. Johnson, *We Hold the Rock: The Indian Occupation of Alcatraz, 1969 to 1971*. San Francisco: Golden Gate National Parks Association, 1997. The story of the Native American occupation of Alcatraz is told through extracts from interviews.

Howard Needham and Ted Needham, *Alcatraz*. Millbrae, CA: Celestial Arts, 1976. Written and illustrated with photographs by two brothers, this book tells the story of life in the Alcatraz penitentiary.

Marilyn Tower Oliver, *Alcatraz Prison in American History*. Springfield, NJ: Enslow, 1998. The author traces the development of the federal prison at Alcatraz Island from its tribal beginnings, Spanish settlements, and military prison to a famous escape-proof prison.

Jay Stuller, *Alcatraz, the Prison*. San Francisco: Golden Gate National Parks Association, 1998. This photo essay was originally printed in the September 1995 *Smithsonian*, as "The Rock."

Websites

Bureau of Prisons (www.notfrisco.com/alcatraz/BOP). The Bureau of Prisons gives the warden's reports for 1934 through 1938, which discuss topics such as preliminary organization, population, administrative staff, power plant, plant operations, boat schedules, discipline, parole, classification, treatment, education, welfare, medical work, industries, mechanical service, and construction work.

National Park Service (www.nps.gov/alcatraz). The National Park Service offers online tours and slideshows entitled "Impressions of Alcatraz," "Indian Occupation," "Prison Life on Alcatraz," "Circumnavigational Tour," "The Military Years," and "Nature on the Rock." Essays and a bookstore are also included.

Works Consulted

Books

Jolene Babyak, *Birdman—the Many Faces of Robert Stroud*. Berkeley, CA: Ariel Vamp, 1994. This meticulously researched biography addresses the myths surrounding Robert Stroud. It includes prison reports, quotes from prisoners, officers, psychologists, and pathologists.

James V. Bennett, *I Chose Prison*. New York: Alfred A. Knopf, 1970. The author was director of the prison bureau from 1937 through 1964. The book examines his work on prison reform, primarily on occupational training.

J. Campbell Bruce, *Escape from Alcatraz*. New York: McGraw-Hill, 1963. Bruce obtained information for this book on the 1962 trio-escape despite a reneged promise of cooperation from James Bennett, director of the Justice Department's Bureau of Prisons.

Don DeNevi, *Alcatraz '46*. San Rafael, CA: Leswing, 1974. The story of the 1946 daring escape attempt is told to DeNevi by officer Philip Bergen and inmate Clarence Carnes. This book uses details obtained from official documents, personal diaries, and interviews with retired Alcatraz personnel and inmates still serving life sentences.

———, *Riddle of the Rock*. Buffalo, NY: Prometheus Books, 1991. DeNevi details the only successful escape from Alcatraz —the Morris-Anglin escape—which occurred in 1962.

Alvin Karpis and Robert Livesey, *On the Rock*. New York: Beaufort Books, 1980. This personal prison story of Alvin Karpis—a twenty-five-year Alcatraz inmate—describes the disregard for humanity and terror perpetuated in the Alcatraz prison.

Paul J. Madigan, *Institution Rules and Regulations*. San Francisco: Golden Gate National Parks Association, 1983. This book, issued to each prisoner, lists fifty-three rules that Alcatraz inmates were required to obey.

Jim Quillen, *Alcatraz from Inside*. San Francisco: Golden Gate National Parks Association, 1991. Through his autobiography, Quillen hoped his book would deter others from the loneliness, fear, heartbreak, and sorrow of prison life.

Leon "Whitey" Thompson, *Alcatraz Merry-Go-Round*. Fiddletown, CA: Winter, 1995. This book continues from *Last Train to Alcatraz*. It tells how Thompson spent twelve more years in and out of prisons after he left Alcatraz. No longer a criminal, Thompson is now an upstanding citizen who, through civic and school presentations and the pre-release prison programs, has had a positive effect on thousands of young lives.

———, *Last Train to Alcatraz*. Fiddletown, CA: Leon W. Thompson, 1988. This autobiography is written by a former Alcatraz convict who served four and a half years on the Rock. It details Thompson's life from childhood through the first year of his release from Alcatraz.

Periodicals

T. H. Alexander, as told by Bryan Conway, "Twenty Months in Alcatraz," *Saturday Evening Post*, February 19, 1938.

Frederick R. Bechdolt, "The Rock," *Saturday Evening Post*, November 2, 1935.

Lora J. Finnegan, "It's Nesting Time on Alcatraz," *Sunset*, April 1993.

Golden Gate National Parks Association, "The Official Map and Guide to Alcatraz," 1991.

Joyce Johnson, "The Grim Corridors of Alcatraz as a Tourist Attraction," *Smithsonian*, October 1975.

Toby J. McIntosh, "Tourists on 'the Rock,'" *Progressive*, March 1975.

Newsweek, "Rock on the Block," April 1, 1963.

Philip O'Farrell, "Alcatraz Prison," *Survey*, January 1934.

Kevin Schafer, "The Real Birdman of Alcatraz," *National Wildlife*, August/September 1987.

Jay Stuller, "There Never Was a Harder Place than 'the Rock,'" *Smithsonian*, September 1995.

Survey, "Is It a Devil's Island?" November 1933.

Edwin H. Sutherland, "America's Devil's Island," *Saturday Review of Literature*, September 10, 1949.

Internet Sources

Sanford Bates, "The Battle Against Crime," 1999. www.notfrisco.com/alcatraz/BOP/Crime33.html.

Department of Justice, "A New Prison," *Alcatraz: The Warden Johnston Years*, November 6, 1933. www.alsirat.com/alcatraz/documents/openpr.html.

Joel Gazis-Sax, "American Siberia: The Purpose of Alcatraz," 1997. www.alsirat.com/alcatraz/purpose.html.

Michael A. Green, "The Creation of Alcatraz," 1998. http://members.aol.com/Beggar21/creal.html.

———, "The Mad Science of Alcatraz," 1998. http://members.aol.com/Beggar21/alcatraz.html.

———"Privileges," 1998. http://members.aol.com/Beggar21/privilege.html.

———, "The Revolutionizing Impact of Johnston's Penology," 1998. http://members.aol.com/Beggar21/johnston.html.

NeySa's Alcatraz Page, "Alcatraz: From Discovery to Demise," 1998. http://pw2.net-com.com/~nely/Alcatraz.html.

Index

A Block cell
location of, 35
solitary confinement in,
42–43
African American convicts,
44, 68–70
Alcatraz (Needham), 50, 64
Alcatraz, Battle of, 75–76
Alcatraz Federal Peniten-
tiary
admitting procedures to,
28–30
arrival on the Rock, 27–28
barrier around, 22
closing of, 90–93
confinement in
prisoners' daily rou-
tines, 46–48
selection of prisoners
for, 19–20, 23
employees at, 22, 78,
84–89
floor plan of, 20
ideal location for, 11,
15–16
new remodeling plans for,
21–22
racial integration at,
43–44, 68–70
relocating inmates from,
93
rules and regulations of,
31, 32–33, 66
wardens at, 19, 85
Alcatraz from Inside
(Quillen), 11, 38, 53
Alcatraz Island
administration of, 97
birds on, 19, 98
civilian population on, 78
lighthouses on, 21

location of, 11, 27–28
Native Americans claim
to, 94–95
ownership of, 10, 14
tourism today, 11, 97–98
transport dock, 28
variety of names, 19
Alcatraz Island Memories
(Hurley), 83
*Alcatraz Prison in American
History* (Oliver), 21
Anglin, Clarence (inmate),
76
Anglin John (inmate), 76
apartments, family, 79–80
armed robbers, 12
Army, U.S., use of island as
military prison, 10, 14,
16
art classes, 64

Babyak, Jolene, 79, 80, 83
bachelor quarters, 78–79
bank robbers, 12
Bates, Sanford
idea of reforming crimi-
nals, 18–19
strategy to separate crime
leaders, 14
B Block cell, 3, 70
Bechdolt, Frederick R., 23
Beechey, Frederick, 19
behavior, code of, 60
Bennett, James V.
on attitudes of inmates,
63
belief in criminal reform,
18, 64
explanation of criminality,
91
on prison officer's first
dilemma, 86

testimony during congres-
sional hearing, 90
black convicts, 44, 68–70
black hole (solitary cell), 39,
40
Blackwell, Olin G. (warden),
84, 85
boat transportation, 80
books and magazines,
48–49, 63
Boyer, LaNada, 94–95, 96
bridge (card game), 58
Broadway corridor, 35, 70
Bruce, J. Campbell
on depression of inmates,
55
on prison work during
World War II, 53
on rebellion by inmates,
67–68
on solitary confinement,
39
bunk beds, 36
Bureau of Prisons (BOP),
role of, 10–11, 13, 23

Capone, Al "Scarface," 18,
32, 61
card games, 58
Carnes, Clarence (inmate),
75
Castillo, Ed, 96
C Block cell
location of, 35
quarantined in, 33, 70
cell blocks
A Block, 42–43
D Block, 37–38
isolation cells, 40, 42
life in the, 36–37, 46–48
location of, 35–36

prisoners choice of, 34
segregation of, 70
solitary cells, 39–40
strip cells, 38–39
cell house
  corridors, 35–36
  hospital, 45
  mess hall, 44–45
  painting of, 45
  safeguard plans for, 22
  see also cell blocks
children, at Alcatraz, 81–83
church services, 61–62
classification counselors,
  33–34
clothing, prison
  abolishment of stripes on,
    19
  restrictions, 33
  uniforms, 29–30, 67
Coast Guard, U.S., 22
college correspondence
  courses, 63
commissary, requests for,
  70–71
contraband, use of, 32, 50,
  72–73
coping with prison, 50, 63
corporal punishment, 19
  see also punishment
correctional officers, 86–89
  see also guards, prison
Coy, Bernard (inmate), 75
Cretzer, Joe (inmate), 75, 77
crime bosses, segregating,
  14
crime rates, U.S., 10–11,
  12–13
criminals, reputation of, 13,
  91
Cummings, Homer S., 14,
  16, 19–20

D Block cell
  isolation cells, 40, 42
  location of, 35

as punishment, 37–38
solitary cells, 39–40
strip cells, 38–39
DeNevi, Don
  on closing Alcatraz, 92
  on code of behavior, 60
  on exercise yard, 59
depression, coping with, 55
Devil's Island, 16
dining halls, 44–45, 50
"Dirty Thirties, the," 12
discipline
  forms of, 34
  isolation cells for, 37–38
  see also punishment
disinfectant, 36, 56
dock tower, 88–89
dungeons, 37

earnings, inmates', 32–33
electrical power, 79–80
Ellis, William J., 15
employees, on Alcatraz, 22,
  84–89
employment, inmate
  on the job, 52–53
  power of, 54–55
  prime jobs, 53–54
  purpose of, 51–52
entertainment, forms of,
  48–49, 63
escape attempts, 74–77
Escape from Alcatraz
  (Bruce), 39, 53
executions, 75
exercise yard, 57–60
Eyewitness on Alcatraz
  (Babyak), 78, 80

families on Alcatraz
  advantages to living on Al-
    catraz, 78–79
  boat transportation, 80
  children's activities, 82–83
  housing, 79–80
  life on the island, 78

recreational activities, 84
school boat schedule,
  81–82
unexpected communica-
  tion with prisoners,
  83–84
Federal Bureau of Investigation (FBI), 13
Federal Prison Industries,
  52
fighting, punishment for, 45
fingerprints, 30
Fish Row, 44
Folsom State Penitentiary, 19
food, prison, 50, 68
Fort Mason dock, 27, 82
*From Alcatraz to the White
  House* (Williams), 98

games, 58
gas chamber, 75
General Services Adminis-
  tration (GSA), 93, 96, 97
Golden Gate National
  Recreation Area
  (GGNRA), 97
good conduct, 18, 32, 63
Great Depression
  crime and criminals dur-
    ing, 10–11, 12–13
Gregory, George (guard),
  72–73
group riots, 66
guard patrols, 88–89
guards, prison
  authority of, 86–87
  job assignments of, 88–89
  ratio of, 22
  shakedowns by, 72–73
  starting salary for, 86–87
  target practice of, 50
guard towers, 22
gun galleries, 35, 89

Harris, George, 64
head counts, 48

Heaney, Frank (guard)
describes
dining room riot, 66
the epidemic of jail-
breaks, 14
first day at work, 70
first job interview,
87–88
harassment by inmates,
87
inmates
attitudes of, 39
shaving procedures
of, 57
work assignments of,
33
life as a correctional officer at Alcatraz, 44
living on the island,
78–79
opinion of Alcatraz, 99
prison security system, 61
sick call, 45
tower duty, 88
hole, the (solitary), 38
holiday celebrations, 64–65
Hoover, Herbert, 13
Hoover, J. Edgar
crack down on gangsters,
13
zero rehabilitation con-
cept, 17–18
hospital facilities, 45
housing. See cell blocks;
families on Alcatraz
Hubbard, Marvin (inmate),
75
hunger strikes, prison,
66–67
Hurley, Donald J., 61–62, 83

I Chose Prison (Bennett),
63, 86, 91
identification number,
prison, 30
industry jobs, 32, 52–53

Inside the Walls of Alcatraz
(Heaney), 14, 44, 61, 70,
87
Institution Rules and Regulations, 30
irons, ankle, 26
isolation cells, 37–38

jailbreaks, 14
Johnson, Troy R., 96
Johnston, James A. (warden)
administrative policies,
20–21
assignment as warden,
19–20, 85
attempt at color psychol-
ogy, 45
changes under, 64
idea of reforming crimi-
nals, 19, 51
response to rebellion by
inmates, 67
speech for new inmates, 30
Justice, U.S. Department of
ownership of Alcatraz Is-
land, 10, 14
remodeling plans, 21
response to criticism, 16

Karpis, Alvin "Creepy"
explains
A Block solitary, 43
Alcatraz's most notori-
ous inmate, 24
Christmas Eve, 64
daily head counts, 48
first weekend night, 49
kitchen jobs, 54
life in the cell, 36–37
racial integration, 68–69
recreation yard, 58
riot incident, 69–70
strip cell, the, 38–39
transfer to Alcatraz,
23–25, 30
Kelly, George "Machine
Gun," 43

Kennedy, Robert F., 92
kitchen jobs, 54
knives, 72

Langer, William, 91
Last Train to Alcatraz
(Thompson), 25
Leavenworth Federal
Prison, 23–25
leisure time. See privileges,
inmate
library, prison, 48–49, 54
lights out, 49–50
lockups, 46, 51

Madigan, Paul J. (warden),
64, 84, 85
mail restrictions, 63
main tower, 89
Marion penitentiary, 99
McDowell (prison ferry-
boat), 80
McIntosh, Toby J., 11
McNeil penitentiary, 25
mealtime, 46, 50
medical facilities, 45
medical technical assistant
(MTA), 45
mess hall, 44–45, 50
metal detectors, use of, 22,
29, 46, 61, 72
Michigan Boulevard corri-
dor, 35
Mockford, Stanley E. (in-
mate), 63
money, forbidden use of, 32,
50
movies, 61
musical instruments, 48–49,
64
mutinies, 72

National Park Service
(NPS), 97, 98
Native Americans

claim Alcatraz Island, 94–95

struggle for political control, 95–96

Needham, Howard
  on contraband, 50
  on relaxed rules and hobbies, 64
  on selection of prisoners, 23

Oakes, Richard, 94, 96
O'Farrell, Philip, 15
Oliver, Marilyn Tower, 21, 63
On the Rock (Karpis), 16, 23, 68

penologist, 11
photos of inmates, 30
Pier Thirty-Nine, 94
posts, armed guard, 88–89
press relations, 92–93
Prisoner's Trust Fund, 32–33
prison rules
  hunger strikes against, 66–67
  maintaining order, 71–73
  riots against, 54–55, 66
prisons, U.S.
  development of, 10–11
privileges, inmate
  arts and music, 48–49, 64
  bathing and shaving, 56–57
  books and magazines, 48–49, 63
  college correspondence courses, 63
  holiday celebrations, 64–65
  mail correspondence, 63
  movies, 61
  recreation yard, 57–60
  religious services, 60–61

visitors, 61–62
working, 51–52
probation and parole, concept of, 10
Prohibition, 10–11, 12
punishment, forms of, 37, 45, 66, 73–74

quarantine unit, 33
Quillen, Jim (inmate)
  describes
    advantages of working, 53
    cells in D Block, 38
    confinement in D Block, 40
    desperation to escape, 74
    experience in isolation, 42
    first day at work, 46
    first visit from parents, 62
    lessons learned from Alcatraz battle, 76
    mess hall procedures, 50
    recreation yard activities, 58
    rehabilitation, 11
    risks at mess hall, 50
    snitch boxes, 72
    solitary confinement, 39, 40
    ten years at Alcatraz, 74
    work assignments, 52–53

racial integration, 43–44, 68–70
radio broadcasts, 64
rebellions by inmates, 54–55, 66–68
recording facility, 64
recreation yard, 57–60
rehabilitation, 18
religious services, 60–61
revolts, prison, 75–76. *See also* rebellions by inmates
Richmond, California, 25
Riddle of the Rock (DeNevi), 59

riots, inmate, 54–55, 66–68
road tower, 89
Rock, the, 23
Rogers, Bill (guard), 86
routines, inmates' daily, 46–48

safety features, 22
San Francisco, California
  concerns of citizens, 15, 16
  doctors and hospitals, 45
  ferries from, 80–82, 97
San Quentin penitentiary, 16, 19
Saturday Evening Post, 29
searchlight towers, 22, 88–89
security, prison, 21–22, 61, 88–89
segregation, race, 43–44, 68–70
Segregation Act (1917), 19
sentences, prison, 19–20, 23, 74
shackles, ankle, 24
shakedowns, cell, 72–73
shaving procedures, 57
Shockley, Sam (inmate), 75, 77
shower privileges, 56–57
sick call, 45
silence rule, 46, 54–55
snitch boxes, 22, 29, 46, 61, 72
Sobell, Morton (inmate), 58
solitary cells, confinement in, 39–40
Speedy Street corridor, 35
sports, 58
Stadig, John (inmate), 39
strikes, prison, 54–55, 66–67, 70–71
strip cells, 38–39
strip searches, 29

Stroud, Robert "Birdman," 40–43
suicide, 21
Sutherland, Edwin H., 23
swimming escapees, 22
Swope, Edwin (warden), 67, 84, 85

Thayer, Walter N. Jr., 15
Thompson, Leon "Whitey"
  as inmate at Alcatraz, 31
  interview for work assign-
    ment, 33–34
  transfer to Alcatraz,
    25–27
Thompson, Miran (inmate),
  75
Times Square corridor, 35
tower patrol, 88–89
transfers to Alcatraz
  of prisoners

from Leavenworth
  23-25
from McNeil Island,
  25–27
selection process, 23
transports, prison, 23, 25–26
treatment unit (UT), 38
Trudell, John, 94, 96

uniforms, prison, 29–30, 33,
  67

visitor restrictions, 61–62
Volstead Act (1920), 12

Warden Johnston (prison
  ferryboat), 27, 80
Warden Madigan (prison
  ferryboat), 80
wardens, at Alcatraz, 84–86
War Department, 14

Weatherman, Frank C. (in-
  mate), 93
weekdays, routines during,
  46–48
weekends, routines during,
  57
We Hold the Rock (John-
  son), 96
whistles, 46
Williams, Nathan Glenn (inmate), 98–99
work assignments, inmate
  daily routine during,
    46–48
  industry jobs, 52–53
  interviewing for, 33–34, 51
  prime jobs, 53–54
  privilege of, 51–52
work strikes, 54–55, 70–71

Yocom, Richard, 45

Picture Credits

About the Author

Judith Janda Presnall was raised in Milwaukee, Wisconsin, and earned a bachelor of education degree from the University of Wisconsin, Whitewater. She taught business classes at high schools and community colleges.

Life on Alcatraz is Presnall's ninth nonfiction book. Lucent Books has published six of her works, including *Mount Rushmore, Oprah Winfrey, The Giant Panda, Artificial Organs,* and *Rachel Carson.* Both the Society of Children's Book Writers and Illustrators and the California Writers Club have recognized Presnall for her nonfiction writing. In 1997 the California Writers Club, San Fernando Valley Branch, honored Presnall with the Jack London Award for meritorious service.

Presnall and her husband, Lance, live in Southern California with their three cats. They have two adult children. Presnall enjoys research traveling and meeting people with a historical background relating to her writing projects.